Praise for *Lean Brands*

"Luis Pedroza provides a generous dose of actionable, approachable global insight vital to any marketer today."

—Mark Schaefer, author of *Marketing Rebellion*

"A must-read for every marketer with global ambitions. Packed with examples, Pedroza reveals how the Ninja approach drives exceptional brand performance. Personal, practical, powerful."

—Thomas Barta, author of *The 12 Powers of a Marketing Leader*

"Throughout my career, I had two colleagues I truly admired. They had something I did not have, so I tried to learn from them. Luis was one of them. When faced with a multitude of hurdles to overcome in introducing breakfast cereals into China, his creative and conceptual thinking were key drivers to leap and break the hurdles. I have incorporated his outlook and capabilities into my own workplace and have truly seen growth in building my marketing career. I am excited to see the impact Luis will make with his book. Filled with his global brand-building experiences, this book will inspire the next generation of global marketers as it did me, when I worked closely with him."

—Yong J. Park, CMO at Coway and former VP of global product marketing at Samsung Electronics

LEAN BRANDS

Catch Customers, Drive Growth & Stand Out in All Markets

LUIS PEDROZA

CAREER
PRESS

This edition first published in 2020 by Career Press, an imprint of
Red Wheel/Weiser, LLC
With offices at:
65 Parker Street, Suite 7
Newburyport, MA 01950
www.redwheelweiser.com
www.careerpress.com

ISBN: 978-1-63265-165-5
Library of Congress Cataloging-in-Publication Data
available upon request.

Cover design by Kathryn Sky-Peck
Interior photos/images by Amy Hsu and Luis Pedroza
Interior by Gina Schenck
Typeset in Avenier Next Condensed and Minion Pro

Printed in Canada
MAR
10 9 8 7 6 5 4 3 2 1

To my family,

To Mom and Dad for believing in me from the very beginning and to my wife, Amy, for supporting me and following me all over the world. To my amazing children, Luis, Michael, and Emily, for all your understanding and always having to share me with my work. You all give me the strength and courage to do what I do.

Acknowledgments

I must begin by thanking Jackie Meyer, my literary agent. Her belief in this project validated my own belief when I needed it the most and fueled my second wind. I would also like to thank PJ Dempsey, who helped me crystalize thinking and create a more persuasive structure, and Professor Dennis Schorr from USC for sparking my interest in this field.

Finally, I would like to acknowledge the many colleagues that encouraged my lean, ninja tendencies throughout the years. I have always sought to surround myself with other crazy thinkers that would inevitably bring out the best in me and elevate the projects that I worked on. So, a big thanks to Pat, Kurt, Pano, and John from the early days. Frank Gambina, I have tremendous gratitude to you for recognizing my passion as I was learning how to lead others. Yong Park, you taught me how to really listen to consumers and listen to my intuition. Patrick Finney, you reinforced my belief that cross-functional collaboration and co-creation is always the preferred route. Paul, Pete, and the rest of the gang at Glanbia, thanks for giving me freedom to refine my thinking around co-creation and strategic marketing. Monika, Eugene, and Prashant, thanks for helping me sharpen my approach to creating synergies and for always bringing intensity and energy to our work. To Abhishek and Gerardo, thanks for charging the hill with me and stretching our paradigm. I have really enjoyed and benefited from working with each of you. Finally, I must thank Michael Pye, Laurie Kelly, Bonni Hamilton, Eryn Eaton, Jane Hagaman, and Kathryn Sky-Peck at Career Press. Their incredible support and assistance made it all happen.

Contents

Part 3: Bring It to Life

The Pre-Journey

"Thank God for the journey."
–James Brown

*"An artist is an explorer. He has to begin by self-discovery and by observation
of his own procedure. After that he must not feel under any constraint."*
–Henri Matisse

remember the exact moment I fell in love with global marketing, when I felt that spark and became fascinated with the art and science behind building strong brands in international markets. That's when I knew that global brand building could be fun, and that I wanted to get in on it.

It was the fall of 1997, and I was taking a graduate course on international marketing at the University of Southern California. On my first day of class, the professor brought in two cans of Classic Coca-Cola. One was from the United States and the other was from Japan. We were asked to examine each can carefully to compare and contrast their differences and hypothesize why changes were made. The professor told us that large global companies did not make changes to their flagship brands without good reason. So, if there were noticeable differences, it was intentional.

I had heard stories about how Coke was formulated using different kinds of sugar and water depending on its place of origin. Growing up in Southern California, I drank Coke made in Mexico and liked it. My friends and I thought Mexican Coke tasted sweeter, probably because Mexico made their Coke with real cane sugar instead of corn syrup. What I didn't realize growing up in the United States was just how big the visual differences could be depending on where the Coke was made.

The first difference I saw when comparing the two cans was how beautiful the Japanese can was. It was smaller than the American can and the printing quality was stunning. The Japanese can looked like glossy red lacquer, and the bottom of the can looked like it was painted white. Conversely, the American can of Coke was much less sophisticated, with pixelated graphics and color that seemed dull by comparison.

At the time, those differences surprised me, but after working in Asia, and specifically Japan, they make perfect sense. The Japanese are known for their attention to detail, with great packaging being mere "table stakes." In fact, any brand launching a new product in Japan must use the highest quality packaging materials just to be considered a credible option by Japanese consumers.

A Japanese Coca-Cola can. Photo credit: Amy Hsu

Fast-forward twenty years and I'm living my dream. I have had the pleasure of building successful brands for a wide range of companies all over the world, and the privilege of living and working in exciting locations such as Beijing, Moscow, Manchester, Singapore, and Shanghai. With each new international assignment, I have expanded my global brand-building toolkit.

Along the way, I learned that global brand builders need to be scrappy. With limited information and resources available to them in developing markets, global brand builders have to do more with less. They need flexibility, speed, and an ability to inspire diverse groups of stakeholders to imagine what is possible. This modus operandi is what I like to call "acting like a ninja," and it's how I built a successful career. It's also why I wrote this book. I wanted to give back and inspire others by sharing the successful techniques and lessons I learned along the way.

A Brand-Building Manual

Lean Brands provides an agile method for building strong brands and helps you make sense of your environment, so you can quickly create a differentiated brand positioning and then bring that strategy to life on the ground where it counts.

My hope is this book becomes your go-to manual on global brand building. You will soon embark on a three-part journey to becoming a lean global brand builder.

- **In Part One, Assemble Your Tool Kit,** you will learn to conduct "recon" on your competition and fight to compete and win against larger, better-resourced opponents.

- **In Part Two, Define Your Strategy,** you'll gain the tools to differentiate your brand based on the real needs of consumers and use lean brand-building techniques to create solutions that solve those needs quickly.

- **In Part Three, Bring It to Life,** you'll see how emerging technology can be leveraged to change the growth trajectory of your brand and discover how to improve the effectiveness of your content by ensuring your communication is on strategy, memorable, and presented in a format that can be easily adapted to meet local needs. You will also learn how to improve the quality of your innovation by merging your intuition with analysis and using ninja-style "creative hacks" to stimulate creative thinking.

Part 1
Assemble Your Toolkit

The Ninja 1

"Ninjas don't wish upon a star, they throw them."
−Jarius Raphel

S o what do ninjas have to do with global brand building? For me, ninja warfare provides a perfect metaphor for the scrappy kind of lean marketing that is required to enter and unlock growth in foreign markets. I am not talking about the way ninjas are typically portrayed in Hollywood, infiltrating enemy lines and assassinating emperors under the cover of night. And, I'm definitely not saying that you need to kill anyone. What I am talking about is getting inside the head of your enemies (your competition) and devising a plan of attack to beat them.

What Do Ninjas Do?

Ninjas practiced Ninjutsu, an ancient form of warfare used in feudal Japan. Ninjutsu required that warriors prepare for battle using a strict methodology that relied heavily on intelligence gathering and strategy creation.[1] Ninja fighters were trained experts in reconnaissance, so they could thoroughly scout an enemy and understand its strengths and weaknesses before exploiting what they had learned to create a competitive advantage.

Jinichi Kawakami is the sixty-seven-year-old head of the five-hundred-year-old Koka ninja clan and teaches a business course at Mie University in Tsu, Japan. According to Kawakami, "Ninja[s] were skilled in many arts, but one of the most important has always been collecting information about your opposition. That is just as important in the world of business today as it was in the feudal era hundreds of years ago."[2]

Ninjutsu is actually a type of guerrilla combat in which smaller groups of faster-moving fighters were able to take advantage of larger, slower-moving armies. That's because established armies, like established brands, tend to be slow and predictable. When entering international markets, global brands are often tempted to replicate their existing structure, brand associations, and value proposition, hoping what worked before will work again. Unfortunately, this kind of wishful thinking is almost always suboptimal because it is predictable, doesn't take advantage of being new, and assumes that the brand will have the same level of support in the new market as it did back home.

Like the global brand builder who is asked to enter a foreign market to compete against larger, more established local brands, ninjas had fewer resources than the established armies they faced. That's why both ninjas and global brand builders benefit from engaging in guerrilla-style, asymmetrical warfare to gain a competitive advantage.[3]

To win in a foreign market, you almost always have to adapt your brand's value proposition to meet the needs of local consumers and stakeholders. Like a ninja, take advantage of the predictability of established brands and learn from their mistakes and weaknesses.

Nestlé China

Nestlé China learned from the earlier mistakes made by Kellogg to improve its launch of breakfast cereals into China.

Early on in my career at General Mills, I accepted an expat assignment in China working for a joint venture between Nestlé and General Mills. I led a successful launch of Nestlé breakfast cereals into China following a failed attempt by Kellogg in the early 1990s.

Kellogg's big mistake was trying to build the cereal category in China the same way it had in the United States in the 1940s. Back then, the popularity of eating breakfast cereal started to grow in America, as companies like Kellogg positioned cereals to adults as a convenient way to eat grains. Grains were known to be nutritious, and breakfast cereals, unlike oatmeal that required cooking, was "ready-to-eat" right out of the box (see Figure 1.1). In the 1950s, Kellogg and General Mills started leveraging the nutritional equity they had built and added more sweetness to appeal to Baby Boomer children.

Following its existing playbook, Kellogg entered China and started targeting adults with unsweetened corn flakes, rice flakes, and wheat flakes positioned as nutritious. However, Chinese adults were not looking for new nutritious breakfast solutions. They already had their traditional Chinese diet.

As my team at Nestlé prepared to enter the breakfast cereal market, we noticed how China's one-child policy had created a nation of single-child families and thought we could use this to our advantage. We discovered that the parents and grandparents of these "little emperors" were extremely motivated to find nutritious breakfast options to help their children grow up healthy. We also found that mothers in China, like their counterparts all over the world, struggled to get their children to eat a nutritious breakfast before sending them off to school. Kids in China were just as picky as kids in America and also enjoyed eating breakfast cereals because of the fun shapes, texture, and sweetness.

So when we launched breakfast cereals into China, it was with an adapted portfolio of nutritious products that we knew Chinese kids would enjoy eating. Our battle cry was "Moms trust it; kids love it." Nestlé breakfast cereals eventually grew to become the category leader in China (see Figure 1.2).

Figure 1.1. Photo of vintage 1951 Cheerios print advertisement.
Photo credit: Amy Hsu

Figure 1.2. Original launch packaging for Nestlé Milk & Egg Stars, 2003.
Photo credit: Amy Hsu

Plan Your Attack

1. Identify the attributes that your competitors are committed to, the ones that would be difficult for them to change. How can you use that immobility to your advantage?

2. Predict how the existing brands in the market will react to your entry. How did they react to new entrants in the past?

3. Study and learn from the mistakes competitors made when entering the market before you.

See the New Battleground 2

"Some people don't like change, but you need to embrace change if the alternative is disaster."

–Elon Musk

B uilding a differentiated brand in a foreign market requires agility. Each time you prepare to enter a new market, you must revalidate your industry assumptions and be willing to reframe your perspective of the competitive landscape. So get ready to unpack your assumptions and prepare to be surprised.

Reframe Your Perspective

The truth is, you can't just flip a switch and change your paradigm. So here is an exercise to help you gain a fresh perspective on your competition. List out the major assumptions that underpin how you operate in your home market. Then, validate that they still apply to the new market you are trying to enter. Pay particular attention to

1. **The Target:** Who are your target users, and what needs does your product solve for them? Do consumers in the new market have the same needs?

2. **Market Size:** How many target users are there in your new market, and what percentage of them will buy your brand? What is the potential size of the prize?

3. **Competitive Environment:** Who are your direct and indirect competitors? Are there barriers to entry? What attributes and benefits do they compete on?

4. **Consumer Purchasing Power:** Do your target consumers have enough money to purchase your product the way it is currently designed? Realistically, how often can they afford to repeat their purchase?

5. **Pricing:** Should you position your brand as a premium or everyday product? Is the price per use aligned to the average income level?

6. **Demographics:** Is the target population growing or in decline? Do factors like age or ethnicity play a role in shaping consumer needs?

7. **Category Lifecycle:** Is the category lifecycle at a different stage of development? If so, how will this affect communication and the appeal of your product's benefits?

8. **Value Chain:** How will your product get distributed to the end-user? Who are the key stakeholders involved in the supply chain and what are their expectations?

Get Ready for Lots of Change

In today's increasingly urbanized, fast-changing environment, entering new markets with properly branded offerings has never been more necessary. On my first trip to Nanjing, China, in 1998, I visited local grocery stores and noticed that most of the products being sold were only offered in bulk-style, clear bags and hardly any had branding. At that time, Nanjing was an emerging, second-tier city in China. When I returned three years later, everything had changed. Not only were there more Western brands on the shelves, but many local brands had become more Westernized by incorporating glossy printed packaging with well-designed, illustrated logos.

Pay Attention to Emerging Cities

In 1990, there were only ten "mega" cities in the world with more than ten million people living in them. Now, the United Nations projects that by 2030, there will be more than forty such "mega" cities globally, and by 2050, 66 percent of the world's population will be living in urban areas.[1]

Beyond well-known megacities like Shanghai, Mumbai, and Mexico City, there are many emerging cities that should be on your radar as you plan for growth. In the past and unfortunately even today, most large companies focused primarily on megacities, leaving emerging cities to be developed by distributors and brokers. According to Boston Consulting Group, by 2030, there will be more than one thousand cities in emerging markets with populations over half a million. That means at least an additional 1.3 billion consumers will be living in emerging market cities, compared to one hundred million new consumers calling existing developed cities their home.

The implications of this change cannot be overstated. To put it into perspective, in 2005, if you wanted to reach 80 percent of China's middle class, you only needed distribution in 60 cities. In 2020, to maintain 80 percent coverage, you need distribution in more than two hundred Chinese cities.[2]

If that weren't challenging enough, the size of emerging market cities is evolving much faster than the behavior and perceptions of the migrants who inhabit them. This results in emerging city consumers with drastically different needs and preferences than those living in the megacities. Although it is not practical for companies to focus on every emerging city, becoming a leaner and more agile brand builder will allow you take advantage of more opportunities.

Take Advantage of Rising Incomes

Income levels are rising across developing markets as workers migrate from rural areas into the cities. In India, for example, 40 percent of the population will be living in urban areas by 2025, and city dwellers will account for more than 60 percent of the country's total consumption.[3] It is expected that this growth will also generate more disposable income and boost demand for branded products and services.

Internet Access Is Changing Demand

Information is power. In fact, there is a strong correlation between Internet access and purchasing power. As workers earn more money, they can afford to buy smartphones and personal computing devices. According to the Pew Research Center, many large emerging economies now have at least 60 percent of their populations using the Internet, including 72 percent in Russia, 68 percent in Malaysia, 65 percent in China, and 60 percent in Brazil.[4]

Thanks to this digital transformation, new urban consumers are seeing how people live in other parts of the world for the first time, and this affects their buying behavior. More access to the Internet also provides more opportunities for companies to reach emerging consumers, making it easier to sell products and services to larger groups of buyers. In 2017, online retail sales in China surpassed one trillion dollars for the first time, with rural areas growing 39 percent compared to 32 percent overall.[5]

Don't Be Afraid of Premium Pricing

Don't assume that you need to lower your price to penetrate emerging markets. Research suggests that after being exposed to a higher standard of living, many new middle-class consumers demand a taste of what they have been missing.[6] According to The Nielsen Company, large numbers of consumers in developing countries are trading up on everyday items like personal care, home care, beauty, and food products. In Asia's developing markets, between 2012 and 2014, premium-tier products (products costing at least 20 percent more than the category average) more than doubled the growth rate of mainstream and value-tier products.[7]

Fish Where You Can Get Full

We all know the expression "Fish where the fish are," but I think this familiar saying needs some tweaking in the context of global brand building. I always tell my teams, "You shouldn't just fish where the fish are, but instead, go where you can catch fish that are big enough to get you full."

According to Mark Johnson, cofounder of Innosight and a global expert on growth strategy, when brands enter emerging markets, they usually go for the extremes.[8] First they go low, focusing all of their energy on lowering costs to make their products affordable for a large population of lower-income consumers. We have all been there, listening to colleagues say things like, "If we could just get one dollar from every person in India, we would be rich." As it turns out, that is an extremely difficult thing to accomplish, because the average Indian consumer only spends about $1.80 USD per day.[9] When brands eventually figure out that they can't make money selling at such low prices, they typically shift gears and go high, this time attacking the very top segment of the market—the small group of wealthy consumers that can actually afford their existing product line. Unfortunately, in the past, the group that most often got ignored by developed market brands was the emerging middle class.

The takeaway is: ignore the middle at your peril. Although we know the needs of the middle class are often not satisfied because they can't afford the high-end products offered by foreign brands, it doesn't mean that they don't desire something better than the low-end products they can afford.

The Five Stages of the Category Lifecycle

Before launching a branded product into a new market, you need to determine the category lifecycle stage. There are five stages:

1. Launch
2. Growth
3. Maturity
4. Decline
5. Renovation

(Renovation is often overlooked but is included because it can drive new category growth and extend the demand curve.)[10]

It's important to remember that consumer needs change depending on the maturity of the category. You should always try to match your value proposition to the category lifecycle stage (see Figure 2.1). The same brand can usually be adapted to satisfy multiple consumer needs. For example, during the early stages of the category lifecycle (launch and growth), many "everyday" products from developed markets (e.g., coffee and ice cream) are successfully repositioned into "special occasion" or premium products when launched in developing markets.

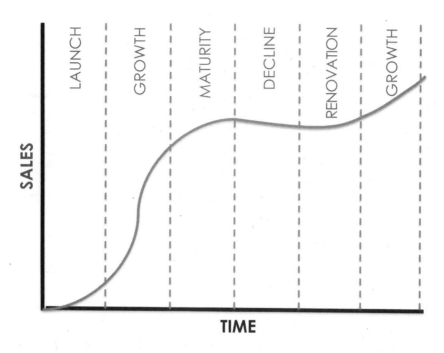

Figure 2.1. Category lifecycle.

Create a Value Advantage

Humans are creatures of habit. To make a change in our behavior and instill a desire to try something new, marketers have to create a wow factor. To get people to stop what they are doing and pay attention, a new branded offering needs to surprise people. The best brands accomplish this by exceeding expectations at each link in the Branded Product Value Chain (see Figure 2.2). When brands exceed expectations, they create what is called a "value advantage."

B2B Insight

Identifying and satisfying a consumer need are not enough to win in a new market. Global marketers must also ensure that store operators and distributors believe that they will be better off selling the new branded offering.

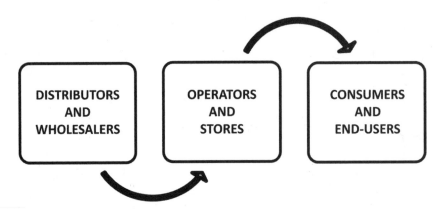

Figure 2.2. Branded Product Value Chain.

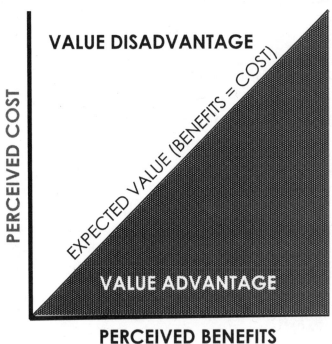

Figure 2.3. Value Advantage is created when perceived benefits exceed perceived costs.[11]

Buick China

Buick captures more demand in China by appealing to a growing and more affluent middle class.

Until very recently, Buick was viewed in the United States as an old brand, driven mostly by retirees. Among younger drivers, the brand was perceived to be tired and dull. These brand associations didn't happen overnight but were built over a long period of time (see Figure 2.4), with the first Buicks manufactured in Flint, Michigan, back in 1903.[12]

In China, however, Buick managed to create a successful new brand image (see Figure 2.5), and there are now more than eight Buicks sold in China for every one sold in the United States. In China, the brand image is considered to be young and vibrant; Buick owners average thirty-five years of age. The brand even manages to outsell Honda, Audi, BMW, and Mercedes-Benz.[13]

A major reason for Buick's success in China is that first-time buyers account for 80 percent of all car purchases.[14] Unlike American buyers who have a strong opinion about their father's Buick, Chinese buyers are more receptive to a new Buick narrative because they don't have strong feelings that need to be overcome. By not anchoring itself to the dated American positioning, Buick was able to appeal to an important younger demographic in China.

Figure 2.4. A 1936 vintage poster advertising Buick cars.
Photo credit: National Motor Museum/Heritage Images/Getty Images

Figure 2.5. A stylish Buick presented at the Shenzhen-Hong Kong-Macao Auto Show. Photo credit: Bartekchiny/Bigstock

Starbucks

Starbucks resonates with today's Chinese consumers by matching its offerings to the category lifecycle stage.

Starbucks has more than 2,800 stores in China and adds roughly 500 new stores each year, making it the fastest growing Starbucks market outside of the United States.[15] As in most developing markets in Asia, the coffee category in China is relatively new and still in the early stages of category development.

Before Starbucks, most Chinese consumers believed Nestlé's Nescafe instant coffee was the gold standard. Nescafe was perceived as Western and purchased primarily for gifting during the Chinese New Year.

Starbucks is considerably more expensive in China compared to the United States. In China, Starbucks is considered a premium offering. The price of a "tall" latte in the United States is roughly $2.75. That same latte in China costs about $4.60. If you factor in differences in income and purchasing power, the gap becomes even wider. The average Chinese worker makes much less than the average American, so when a Chinese consumer buys a "tall" Starbucks latte for $4.60, it actually feels like they are spending more than $7.00.[16]

Figure 2.6. Starbucks Roastery, Shanghai. Photo credit: Amy Hsu

Figure 2.7. Starbucks strawberry yogurt limited time offer, Seoul. Photo credit: Amy Hsu

Figure 2.8. Starbucks LTO table menu coaster, China. Photo credit: Amy Hsu

You notice the difference between American and Chinese coffee culture by observing the store traffic in Starbucks. In America, the morning is the busiest time of day as customers line up for their habitual jolt of caffeine at the same time and location every day.

In China, the busiest time of day for Starbucks is the afternoon. That's when stores are filled with women sipping on dessert-style beverages and taking selfies with their drinks and friends. For these consumers, the coffee shop experience is about entertainment and experiencing an affordable luxury moment. Many of these ladies might never be able to take a trip to America, but they can, from time to time, afford to buy a cup of American coffee.

The differences don't end there, however. Just as Americans don't go to the movies to watch the same film every week, the specialty coffee drinker in Asia doesn't want to drink the same beverage every visit. As a result, in China and many parts of the developing world, the pace of innovation is fast. Large coffee chains in China typically introduce about thirty limited time offers (LTO) every year. Throughout Asia, the bestselling new drinks typically include an ingredient backstory, are Instagram/Weibo worthy (presented with visual "wow"), and incorporate multiple layers of tastes and textures (see Figures 2.6, 2.7, and 2.8 on pages 24–25).

Häagen-Dazs

Häagen-Dazs creates a value advantage by exceeding consumer expectations.

Häagen-Dazs operates hundreds of boutique-style ice cream shops throughout Asia that are modeled after European patisseries, with approximately 380 of them located in eighty-four Chinese cities.[17]

To help elevate quality perceptions, these upscale shops are intentionally placed in shopping areas populated by Western luxury brands. Häagen-Dazs sells beautifully decorated desserts and social media–worthy drinks, all served in an aspirational environment (see Figures 2.9, 2.10, and 2.11).[18]

In Asia's developing markets, the brand has exceeded the expectations of a growing middle-class by adapting its global platforms to appeal to local tastes. In China, flavors like Yuzu Citrus, Mango Snow Slush, and ice cream mooncakes strike the right balance between adaptation and standardization.

Figure 2.9. Exterior of a modern Häagen-Dazs ice cream store in Shanghai, China. Photo credit: Amy Hsu

Figure 2.10. A beautifully plated seasonal dessert at Häagen-Dazs in China. Photo credit: Amy Hsu

Figure 2.11. A Häagen-Dazs shop in Taipei. Photo credit: Amy Hsu

Reposition to Create a Better Local Offering

The two most common arguments for strictly adhering to a global brand positioning when entering a new market are: 1) creating financial and operational efficiencies; and 2) increasing synergies across a global organization. However, neither of these arguments matters much if the current global positioning is weak or doesn't resonate with local consumers.

In these situations, the best option is to reposition the brand to compete in the new market. Finding out that your current global positioning won't work before you launch can be a blessing in disguise. You can take the opportunity to create an improved value proposition, one that leverages the strengths of your global brand equity while minimizing local weaknesses.

One of the big differences between launching an existing brand in an established market and launching a new brand for a developing market is the awareness level of the brand. When you launch a new brand into a new market, consumer awareness of your brand will almost certainly be low. That means you have the freedom to create the perfect offering and take advantage of the incumbent's inability to quickly adapt.

DaVinci Gourmet Asia

DaVinci Gourmet used the brand's low awareness as an opportunity to create a new brand positioning in Asia.

In 2015, I was hired to lead the APAC brand organization for Kerry, the global owner of the DaVinci Gourmet brand. Kerry purchased this American brand in 2003 and had done very little positioning work since (see Figure 2.12). My job was to help Kerry grow the brand in Asia and make a serious run at the global beverage syrup leader, Monin.

Monin, a family-owned French company, has been making and selling beverage syrups for more than one hundred years. The brand uses a vintage-style bottle design along with a very literal ingredient story. For example, Monin names its syrups using direct French translations of the main ingredients (e.g., Pomme Verte for Green Apple) and decorates its bottles with the kind of literal illustrations you would typically find printed in a vintage provincial French cookbook (see Figure 2.13).

There were many changes underway in the coffee industry at the time I joined Kerry. The coffee category in Asia was at the beginning of what many in the industry referred to as the "third wave." The first wave was driven by the convenience of home-brewed and instant coffee options like Folgers and Nescafe, while the second wave was fueled by chains like Starbucks elevating coffee's taste and quality perceptions for the masses. The third wave is about leveraging the entire sensory experience of drinking coffee, often using modern and scientific techniques to extract the goodness that comes from single-origin coffee beans.

Figure 2.12. Global DaVinci gourmet packaging.
Photo credit: Aleksei Isachenko/ Shutterstock

Because Monin was the global leader and the brand most often used by professional bartenders and drink makers, other syrup manufacturers started to gravitate toward Monin and emulating its image. This movement resulted in fewer choices for professional drink makers searching for a more contemporary offering.

Figure 2.13. Monin global syrup packaging.
Photo credit: Gary Perkin/Shutterstock

My team gained insight from dividing the competitive setup based on how traditional and literal each brand's communication was perceived by end-users. After placing all the competitors on a perceptual map, we exposed a gap in the modern/sensorial quadrant (see Figure 2.14).

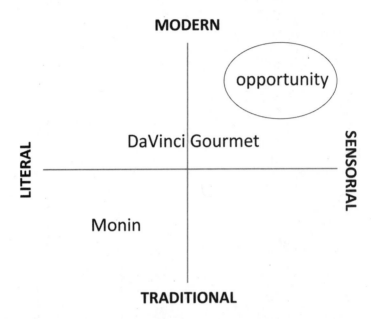

Figure 2.14. Professional beverage syrup perceptual map.

Most coffee shops display their syrup bottles on the counter. My team knew that if a coffee shop wanted to communicate a contemporary sensorial image to its consumers, it would not have many syrup options available to help tell that story. At the time, awareness of the DaVinci Gourmet brand in Asia was very low, and the existing global brand positioning was perceived by end-users as being generic or "middle of the road." So we repositioned the DaVinci Gourmet brand as the contemporary and more sensorial alternative to Monin's traditional and literal brand positioning in Asia (see Figures 2.15 and 2.16).

We knew that Monin had invested so much into establishing its traditional positioning that it would never feel comfortable drastically changing that cultivated image. We quickly redesigned every element of the DaVinci Gourmet brand and made sure that every touch point including the bottle structure, label design, and trade promotions communicated the same new contemporary and highly sensorial positioning.

Figure 2.15. Repositioned DaVinci Gourmet packaging.
Photo credit: Kerry Group, used with permission

Figure 2.16. Repositioned DaVinci Gourmet packaging.
Photo credit: Kerry Group, used with permission

Plan Your Attack

1. Identify ways to take advantage of demographic changes to fuel your brand-building efforts.

2. Adapt your brand's value proposition to meet the category life-cycle needs of the market you are entering.

3. If you are entering a market where the awareness of your brand is low, take the opportunity to reposition your brand instead of following a "one-size-fits-all" strategy.

Know Yourself, Know Your Enemy 3

"The fight is won or lost far away from witnesses—behind the lines, in the gym and out there on the road, long before I dance under those lights."
–Muhammad Ali

"Know yourself, know your enemy, and you shall win a hundred battles without loss."
–Sun Tzu, *The Art of War*

love the expression "punching above your weight." It means fighting enemies that are much larger and better resourced. The ability to fight and win against larger opponents requires not only thorough preparation, but also an obligation to really understand your enemy before engaging in an attack.

The best way to do this is to put aside your own beliefs and assumptions and put on your competitor's "hat." Adopt the perspective of the competitive brand as your brand, and answer each of the following questions:

◆　What products do you make and what problems do they actually solve for the consumer?

◆　What resources are required to produce and distribute the products you manufacture?

◆　For what reasons have you chosen to solve the consumer problem in this specific way?

Construct a Competitive Blueprint

This exercise will explain the value of using a competitive blueprint to understand your competition. If you want to understand exactly how a building is constructed, you analyze the building's structural blueprint. When it comes to your competitor, you can do the same thing by using this simple framework to "unpack" a brand's "Competitive Blueprint" (see Figure 3.1).

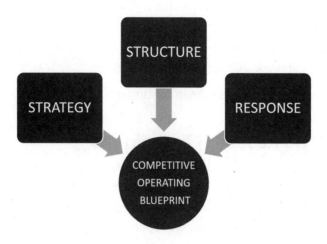

Figure 3.1. Competitive Blueprint framework.

The following three sections are meant to give you a more granular understanding of your competition. Answer them by putting yourself in their shoes.

Brand Strategy

- What would you do next if you managed the brand?
- What do you see as the brand's long-term objectives and strategies?
- What are the brand's strengths and weaknesses?
- Is the brand growing or declining?
- What are the key issues that need to be addressed to grow sales and profits?

Company Structure

- What is the organizational structure?
- How are products distributed to the end-user?
- Who are the key stakeholders?
- What is your estimate of the cost structure?
- How does the brand make money?

Response to Competition

+ How will the brand respond to a competitive launch?
+ What actions will it take to protect sales?
+ What actions will it take to minimize a new entrant's success?

Ninja-Style Research Techniques

I am a big fan of scrappy, ninja-style, guerrilla research. A lot of good work can be performed very quickly on your own, and at a fraction of what a full-service agency will charge. Even if you decide to use an agency, I have found that you can often reduce the scope and cost of custom research just by doing some of your own prework.

The following list of ninja research techniques is not all encompassing, but it does include many popular ways to uncover insights on your own.

Desk Research

Competitive websites often publish digital brochures that contain descriptions of their products and services and provide a broad overview of the local landscape. Online industry magazines and communities also publish lots of relevant information regarding product performance and trends.

Syndicated Data

Depending on the market you are trying to enter, you may be able to purchase existing research reports from companies such as Mintel and Euromonitor who collect and then summarize data that has broad appeal. These "off-the-shelf" reports provide macro-level category reviews along with industry trends and key issues that the industry faces as a whole.

Interviews

Conducting intercept interviews with consumers is a great way to learn more about your target. It's easy to recruit respondents near the point of purchase (e.g., in front of cafes, on the street, and in shopping malls).

Additionally, you can gain valuable insights by arranging informational interviews with industry professionals. Make sure you ask permission to video record your interviews. Verbatim clips of real consumers and distributors can provide powerful support for your internal presentations.

Immersions

One of my favorite marketing activities is participating in local market immersions. Like a cultural anthropologist, you get to immerse yourself into the consumer environment and watch how real end-users interact with various brands. Whether you visit restaurants, grocery stores, or fashion boutiques, you can cover large sections of a city in a single day. Make sure to take lots of pictures and videos of what you see. You will be able to use this content later when you develop your positioning boards and tell your brand story to others.

Online Surveys

Today, there are many cloud-based survey tools that you can choose from to help you generate insights. Companies like SurveyMonkey make it easy to quickly create a questionnaire and field it using their online panel of respondents. Many online survey companies now have global partners to support international research projects.

Apple

Apple uses lean, ninja-style research techniques to quickly understand and adapt to emerging consumer needs.

Steve Jobs once said that Apple did not do market research and followed it up by saying that it didn't hire consultants either. Although that may have been true, Apple certainly uses marketing research now to help make better decisions. In fact, Apple has become very adept at using lean research techniques to gain insights about what consumers want and how they feel about Apple products.

As all Apple users know, an Apple ID is required to access products like iCloud, iTunes, and the App Store, which allows the company to collect data

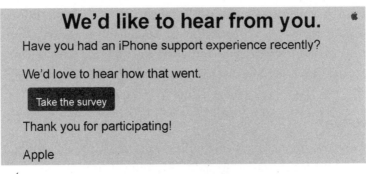

We'd like to hear from you.

Have you had an iPhone support experience recently?

We'd love to hear how that went.

Take the survey

Thank you for participating!

Apple

How did Scarlett do?
Rate your shopping experience at the Apple Store.

Poor   Excellent

(1)   (2)   3   (4)   (5)

Click or tap to answer, and then continue taking the survey.

We love feedback.

Tell us about your experience with iPad.

Take the survey

Your responses will remain completely confidential
and results will be reported only in aggregate.

Please rate your satisfaction in the following areas.

	Totally unsatisfied 1	2	3	4	Very satisfied 5
The simplicity of the purchase process	◯	◯	◯	◯	◯
Get assistance within a reasonable time	◯	◯	◯	◯	◯
How helpful the entire retail shop team is to you	◯	◯	◯	◯	◯

Back   Next Step

Figure 3.2. Apple online survey invitations and requests for consumer feedback. Photo credit: Amy Hsu

to "see" purchasing behavior. Apple uses its Customer Relationship Management (CRM) system to send surveys to customers that gauge satisfaction and help Apple develop better products (see Figure 3.2). While discussing these surveys, Greg Joswiak, the VP of product marketing for Apple, said, "The surveys reveal, country-by-country, what is driving our customers to buy Apple's iPhone products versus other products such as the Android products that Samsung sells, what features they most use, our customers' demographics and their level of satisfaction with different aspects of iPhone."[1]

Another way Apple uses research is watching consumers as they shop. With its new store designs, Apple intentionally created community-gathering spaces where consumers feel free to play with products.[2] Apple merchandises products to optimize this kind of interaction. Additionally, the company offers lots of educational sessions, workshops, and product demonstrations that provide opportunities to listen and learn from its consumers. Today, 64 percent of the store headcount is service focused, dedicated to answering questions and educating customers (see Figures 3.3 and 3.4).[3]

Figure 3.3. People shopping inside an Apple store in Shanghai, China.
Photo credit: Siempreverde22 | Dreamstime

Figure 3.4. Product merchandising inside an Apple store in Hong Kong.
Photo credit: Tea|Dreamstime

Angela Ahrendts, senior vice president for Apple Retail, wrote about the company's free training sessions offered in Apple stores called Today at Apple. These sessions are open to everyone and focus on topics ranging from computer basics to creative passions. In a letter addressed to her team, Ahrendts wrote, "We'll start collecting this type of feedback from everyone who attends a Today at Apple session. We'll focus both on their immediate experience and on their perceptions about the long-term value. We want to be as rigorous in measuring our human impact as we are in every other part of our business."[4]

Mondelēz

Mondelēz uses lean research techniques to quickly test advertising and make adjustments to maximize sales.

Mondelēz is a multinational food company operating in 165 different countries around the world. Some of the company's most famous brands include Oreo, Nabisco, and Cadbury.

In Brazil, Mondelēz conducted lean research to help launch its new apple and cinnamon belVita breakfast biscuit. In order to create and test content quickly, Mondelēz chose YouTube as the primary communication medium for introducing the brand. Using Google Brand Lift analytics allowed Mondelēz to get a very quick read on its initial ad and make rapid improvements.

Google found that retention dropped considerably after only five seconds of viewing the first version of the ad. Using a short online questionnaire and Google search data, Mondelēz was able to make improvements that increased recall by 57 percent and brand awareness by 26 percent compared to the original version.[5]

Size Matters

Before too long, stakeholders will ask you to estimate the size and growth potential of any new business. Figuring out the "size of prize" is one of the first things you need to do when entering a new market. If the opportunity is large enough, you will most likely get approval to spend resources to position and launch your brand.

However, like a ninja warrior without a big army, you probably will not have enough data to make you feel completely comfortable. If the current size of the market is not large enough to warrant having a large research agency like Nielsen or TNS collect and publish syndicated data, you will need to get creative and comfortable extrapolating estimates from the facts that you are able to gather.

Triangulate to See the Size of the Prize

When working with scarce data to estimate the "size of the prize," the margin of error can be unacceptably high. A good way to help validate the accuracy of your estimate is to "triangulate" (see Figure 3.5).

Triangulation is a fairly simple technique that is easily mastered and can help estimate the size of an opportunity. It works by using calculations derived from three different perspectives and then reconciles any differences to arrive at a "reasonable" approximation for the "size of prize."

Figure 3.5. Triangulation framework.

The following are the three approaches that I use most often when applying this method. Each approach starts at a different point to arrive at an estimate.

Bottom-Up Method

In the standard supply chain sequence, product is produced at the manufacturer, and then moves through distribution before finally arriving at an end-user for consumption (see Figure 3.6).

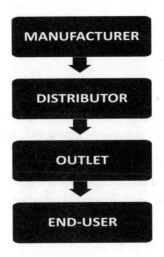

Figure 3.6. Standard supply chain sequence.

Figure 3.7. Bottom-up method.

A Bottom-up approach begins by estimating the number of end-users in your target market, after which you assign a sales rate (trial and repeat) per user to predict a total demand (see Figure 3.7).

Estimate the number of end-users from general to specific. First, approximate the size of a general population that includes your target. For example, you could start by searching for the number of households or families living in a geographic location. Government census bureaus and cross-national organizations like the World Bank and the United Nations regularly publish this kind of data and it can be easily found online for free.

Next, cut the large general population down to a smaller, specific subset that represents the actual target. For example, after you determine the number of households in a city, you could then look at the percentage of above-average income households with children living in that city. If your target is defined by demographic or geographic data, you should be able to use the same data sources mentioned previously.

If your target is defined by purchase behavior, try using a proxy as a substitute. A proxy is a company that sells a product or service to the same target market that you are pursuing. For example, if you want to sell nutritious beverages to children, you could search for a proxy that sells nutritious kid snacks instead.

Use desk research to find data published about the proxy in annual reports and industry articles. You might have to back into some of your numbers. For example, you can estimate the number of consumers a brand has by simply taking annual sales and dividing by an estimate of how much an average consumer buys each year. Once you approximate the size of your target market, you can make an educated guess regarding potential trial and repeat rates for your brand to arrive at your "bottom-up" volume estimate.

Top-Down Method

The top-down approach begins at the distributor level and moves down the supply chain sequence to arrive at an opportunity size. The first step is predicting how many distributors you expect to carry your brand. Then, estimate how much product each distributor can reasonably sell. A great way to obtain distributor information without investing in expensive research is to conduct your own informational interviews with professionals who have extensive knowledge about the market and industry you are trying to enter.

When you feel comfortable with your estimated number of distributors who will sell your brand, you can approximate the number of stores an average distributor covers. Then, assign a reasonable sales volume estimate per outlet to determine your "top-down" projection (see Figure 3.8).

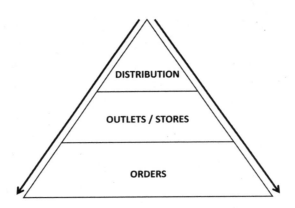

Figure 3.8. Top-down method.

Fair Share

The fair share approach starts in the middle by estimating or obtaining a competitor's market share or sales volume and then uses that figure to extrapolate out to the size of the category and your potential "fair" share.

High-level sales and growth figures can be found in annual reports and industry articles. A scrappy method for estimating competitive market share is to conduct your own small-scale store audits. Randomly select stores that serve your target market. During store visits, take note of which competitors are being sold and ask store employees to tell you how the various brands are performing. Which brands are the most popular? How many units do they sell each day?

You should also study previous launches in the industry. When you know how other new brands performed in the past, it provides a good "sanity" check. When you feel good about your estimate of the competitor's market share, you can then make some reasonable assumptions regarding the total market size and your brand's "fair share" (see Figure 3.9).

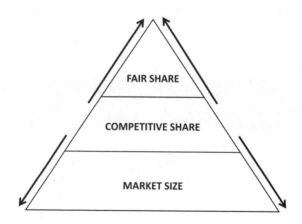

Figure 3.9. Fair Share method.

Deconstruct Your Growth Potential

Beyond calculating the size of the prize, stakeholders and investors want to understand the growth potential for your brand. When you are comfortable with the accuracy of your base volume (size of prize) estimate, you can then apply an annual growth rate to forecast sales out across subsequent years.

A helpful technique for conceptualizing changes in sales volume from one year to the next is the Sales Deconstruction method. Start by pulling out each component or "building block" that makes up your sales growth. Then analyze each factor's contribution separately before reassembling the pieces back together to build a comprehensive forecast (see Figure 3.10). This process will also help determine if your plan will not deliver your intended results, which gives you an opportunity to isolate volume building blocks to make corrections to the plan.

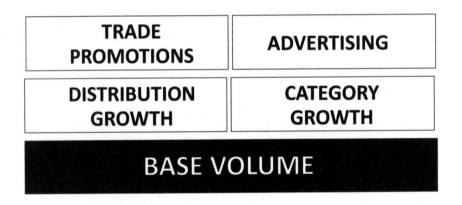

Figure 3.10. Sales Deconstruction method.

Sales Deconstruction

Start with the base volume (size of prize) estimate. Then, build up the expected sales growth, piece by piece. Assign incremental volume to each building block using assumptions taken from your marketing plan. This granular approach will help you justify the investments needed to execute the growth plan.

Plan Your Attack

1. Know your enemy by getting inside its head. Use the Competitive Blueprint Framework to assume the perspective of your competitor.

2. Deconstruct your potential growth to identify growth drivers. Then, design initiatives to stimulate incremental volume.

3. Use lean research techniques to quickly validate your growth plan and share findings to motivate stakeholders.

Part 2
Define Your Strategy

Get Lean and Mean 4

"That's been one of my mantras—focus and simplicity. Simple can be harder than complex: You have to work hard to get your thinking clean to make it simple. But it's worth it in the end because once you get there, you can move mountains."

–Steve Jobs

"A guerrilla is on his own. All you have is a rifle, some sneakers and a bowl of rice, and that's all you need—and a lot of heart."

–Malcolm X

The world may feel like it's getting smaller, but the amount of complexity facing global brands is only becoming larger. Developing and emerging economies are growing twice as fast as developed ones.[1] Much of that growth is fueled by the higher standard of living that comes along with rural-urban migration. It's estimated that by 2025, there will be an additional one billion new consumers living in emerging cities.[2] Global brand builders need to be receptive to seeing the changes that are happening and develop the speed and agility needed to navigate the added complexity.

This emerging consumer class values innovation. According to Nielsen's Global New Product Innovation Survey, more than half of the respondents in Asia-Pacific (69 percent), Africa/Middle East (57 percent), and Latin America (56 percent) claim to have purchased a new product during their last grocery shopping trip, compared with only 44 percent of European and 31 percent of North Americans.[3]

To succeed in this kind of dynamic environment in which emerging market consumers have a voracious appetite for innovation, global brand builders need to find ways to connect the dots faster to create value propositions that will meet the needs of these growing populations.

One Size Does Not Fit All

Think again if you believe that you can create pan-regional products that will satisfy all of the countries in a given region. A single region like Asia-Pacific (APAC), for example, consists of roughly twenty-seven countries. To compete effectively, you need to employ a lean process that can help you identify local needs and develop differentiated value propositions quickly.

Figure 4.1 illustrates why it is difficult to create pan-regional products. If you look at the four largest markets in Asia (Japan, South Korea, China, and Indonesia), you will see how little they have in common. In fact, they are drastically different in terms of median age, average income, education, and religion.

NOT THE SAME

	JAPAN	S. KOREA	CHINA	INDONESIA
MEDIAN AGE	46	41	37	28
MONTHLY WAGE (USD)	2,815	3.405	515	183
YRS. EDUCATION	9.5	11.7	6.4	5.0
MAIN RELIGION	Shinto	Christianity	Buddhism	Islam

Sources: Gallop Worldwide, Median Household Income , worldmeters, Nationmaster

Figure 4.1. Asians consumers are not all the same.

Brands Matter

In my experience, even when shopping for basic necessities in an emerging market, quality is not always guaranteed; that's why brands matter. David Aaker writes that brands are "an organization's promise to a customer to deliver what the brand stands for."[4]

According to GfK's Roper Reports, 79 percent of developing Asian market consumers and 61 percent of Latin American consumers "only buy products and services from a trusted brand."[5] This buying behavior is also supported by a McKinsey & Company study that found strong brands increasingly outperform the market (see Figure 4.2).[6]

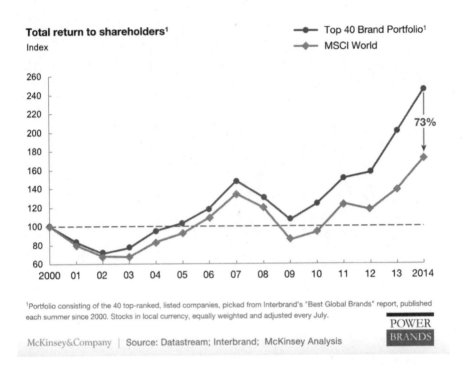

Figure 4.2. Strong brands increasingly outperform the market. Copyright 2018 McKinsey & Company. All rights reserved. Reprinted with permission

Reverse Innovation

Innovation is absolutely critical to global brand building. Essentially, an entire product portfolio can be categorized as new when entering an international market.

There was a time when global marketing basically meant taking standardized products that were designed for developed markets and trickling them down to developing markets, but that has changed. The traditional model has been turned on its head as more and more companies are starting to reverse the flow. Now we see that innovation efforts for local markets can have a much wider global impact on a company's total sales.

This is best described as "reverse innovation," a term made popular by Vijay Govindarajan, a professor at the Tuck School of Business who is widely regarded as one of the world's leading experts on strategy and innovation.[7] The idea behind reverse innovation is that game-changing ideas will increasingly come via developing markets where brands must be more nimble, faster, and innovative to deliver profitable growth. Consider the following examples:

◆ Leveraged Freedom Chair (LFC) is a wheelchair manufactured in India that is designed specifically for people in developing countries. It is 80 percent faster and 40 percent more efficient than a conventional wheelchair and sells for only $250, making it similarly priced to other developing world offerings.[8] As a result, LFC's innovative design principles are now being applied to wheelchair offerings in developed markets as well.

◆ General Electric's MAC 400 and MACi are ultra-portable electrocardiogram (ECG) machines designed and manufactured in India. They are less than one-third of the price of imported ECG machines of similar quality. Because of their compact design, these models are also selling well in developed regions like Europe as an innovative solution for first responders.[9]

◆ Xiaomi, a Chinese mobile phone company, started producing low-cost phones in 2010 specifically for the China market. Xiaomi offers phones that compete with Apple and Samsung but at half the price. By focusing efforts on delivering high quality, low cost, and attractive designs, Xiaomi is finding success in other markets beyond China. Notably, it's now the fourth largest mobile phone company in China, and it recently became India's number-one mobile phone with $1 billion in annual sales. Xiaomi's current plans include opening an additional two thousand stores throughout the next three years in more than forty markets around the world.

Stage-Gate Approach

Stage Gate (Phase Gate) refers to a product management technique that requires product concepts to pass through distinct go/no-go gates before a product is allowed to launch. It works like this: When a project team completes a phase of work and reaches a gate, the team must obtain approval before the project can move forward (see Figure 4.3).

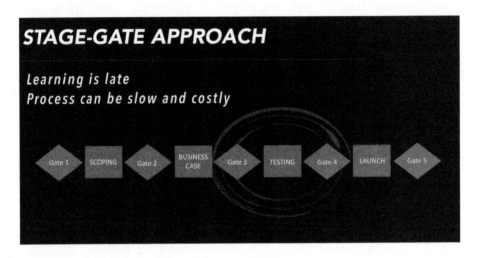

STAGE-GATE APPROACH

Learning is late
Process can be slow and costly

Gate 1 — SCOPING — Gate 2 — BUSINESS CASE — Gate 3 — TESTING — Gate 4 — LAUNCH — Gate 5

Figure 4.3. Stage-gate approach.

Most companies use some form of a stage-gate process to help them manage their innovation workstream. While the linear nature of the approach appeals to many managers, the straightforwardness can provide a false sense of security. Even though most companies embrace a stage-gate approach, at least 85 percent of new fast-moving consumer goods (FMCG) will fail in the marketplace.[10]

A major drawback of the stage-gate approach is that consumer validation typically doesn't happen until the end, when it is less actionable and after considerable resources have already been spent. Stage-gate projects are also notoriously slow to reach the market. Designed like a relay race, development can often take years to complete, depending on the complexity of the concept.

The Lean Approach

A lot of great books have been written regarding lean approaches and their usefulness in all kinds of business situations, ranging from tech startups to design projects to product manufacturing. Eric Ries, author of *The Lean Startup*, describes his popular methodology as "validated learning."[11]

According to Ries, entrepreneurs should not begin their journey by writing detailed hypothetical business plans, but instead create a list of their best guesses of what they believe will work and then quickly test their hypotheses.

To borrow a phrase from Steve Blank, the author of *The Startup Owner's Manual*, when brand builders are constructing a value proposition, they should "get out of the building" to test their hypotheses and get feedback from real consumers in real-life situations.[12] That way, they can make quick use of their learning and refine their hypotheses as needed.

I adapted Eric Ries's Lean Startup methodology by creating a simple four-step process, which I use to launch new products in international markets (see Figure 4.4).

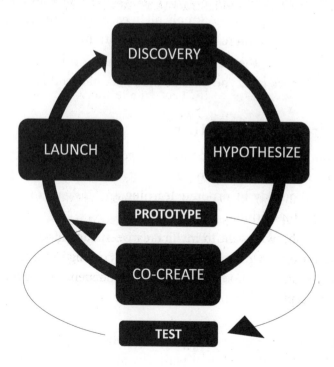

Figure 4.4. The four-step lean brand development process.

Step One: Discovery

Discovery is where you will uncover what motivates your target consumers and identify their unmet needs. It's how you gain a clear understanding of the competitive environment and assess your company's strengths and weaknesses versus the competition. It's also the perfect occasion to use lean research techniques to find gaps in the solutions currently available to your target.

Step Two: Hypothesize

When you hypothesize, you take the insights you uncovered in discovery and build a differentiated value proposition that you will test later in co-creation. You can see the Lean Brand Canvas template in Figure 4.5. This canvas was adapted from Ash Maurya's one-page lean canvas and has been optimized specifically for global brand building.[13] You will find that it is an easy-to-use template for clearly laying out each brand building block and its corresponding hypotheses. Simply fill in each box of the canvas with the hypotheses that you want to validate in co-creation.

Start by defining the target market and then work your way through each building block until you have defined the total product offering.

Step Three: Co-Creation

Co-creation is designed to help rapidly develop prototypes alongside consumers and industry experts to get instant feedback and validation. Your objective is to quickly incorporate learning and insights to improve your brand's value proposition.

Naturally you will want to invite creative stakeholders like marketers, designers, and agency partners to attend your co-creation sessions with the consumers. It will be important to also include some product developers and those responsible for manufacturing your product to ensure your concepts are feasible.

Because co-creation sessions are relatively quick to organize and execute, you should repeat sessions with new recruits until you feel confident you have validated the value proposition or need to pivot (change direction) and create new hypotheses to test.

1. TARGET	2. KEY INSIGHT	3. POSITIONING
• Who is the product gatekeeper? • Who is the actual end-user? • Who are the influencers and opinion leaders?	• What are the Accepted Consumer Beliefs that can be leveraged when creating solutions? • What are the real needs that consumers are trying to solve when choosing between brands?	• How is the brand different vs. the competition? • What is the gap that your brand can own in the mind of the consumer?

4. PROMISE	5. ETHOS	6. STORY
• What are the emotional and rational benefits that the brand promises to provide to end-users? • What are the key brand associations that reinforce that promise?	• What does the brand stand for? • What are the beliefs that the brand lives by? • What is the internal compass that guides to the brand to meet the brand's promise?	• What is the narrative that explains the "reasons to believe" that the brand can deliver on the positioning and promise? • What are the emotional and conceptual mechanics that support the brand story?

7. EXPERIENCE	8. VALUE
• How does the target market experience the brand? • How does brand come to life at each touch point?	• Identify the value chain needed to deliver the branded product/solution to the end user. • How does the branded product/solution exceed value expectations at each link of the value chain to deliver on the brand experience?

9. PRODUCT

• Clearly define the total product offering:

• Product	• Distribution	• Promotions
• Pricing	• Communication	• Service

• Make sure each product element brings the Lean Brand Canvas strategy to life
• Each element should work together to create synergy and consistency

Figure 4.5. Lean Brand Canvas.

Deutsche Post (DHL) Group

DHL co-creates with key customers to improve its value proposition and drive incremental growth.

In 2017, DHL reported its eighth consecutive quarter of record-breaking results. A large contributing factor was the growth generated from international expansion and a strategic focus on high-growth sectors like international e-commerce.[14]

DHL uses innovation workshops to co-create with customers when it enters new markets because "The workshops provide the opportunity to share best practices, explore industry and cross-industry use, and examine the future of logistics. In these workshops, the customer and DHL are jointly engaged in developing ideas for new products, services, or processes."[15]

The following list includes a few innovations that have come out of DHL co-creation sessions that have the potential to step-change DHL's growth trajectory.[16]

- **Smart glasses:** Augmented reality technology for DHL workers that improves inventory and warehouse picking efficiency by 25 percent.

- **Maintenance on Demand (MoDe):** Sensors automatically relay delivery vehicle and component performance to identify when and where truck maintenance will be required.

- **Parcelcopter:** A drone delivery service to deliver parcels to remote areas and help businesses become more efficient and responsive (see Figure 4.6).

- **Robotics applications:** Robots ranging from self-driving trolleys to robots that support pickers and copacking (see Figure 4.7).

Figure 4.6. DHL Parcelcopter.

Figure 4.7. DHL Robotics: Sawyer 02. Source: Deutsche Post AG

Kerry Group

Kerry co-creates with key opinion leaders to test prototypes and applications before launching them into the wider market.

I led the development of a new range of professional drink-making products for Kerry Group that became the foundation for the repositioning of the DaVinci Gourmet brand by elevating taste and quality perceptions among professional drink makers.

My team used the Lean Brand Development process from beginning to end. We organized co-creation sessions throughout the region, inviting well-known bartenders and baristas to join us at central locations. At these sessions, we shared prototypes with professional drink makers and encouraged them to play with the prototypes (hypothetical products) and test them in real drink applications.

The participants would create their own drink recipes using the prototypes provided, and then immediately share what they liked and didn't like with our cross-functional team of marketers and product developers. We would then take their feedback and use it to improve the prototypes on the spot. Afterward, we repeated this exercise in other markets throughout the region.

Every time we conducted subsequent co-ceation sessions, the performance of the prototypes improved considerably. After only a few months of work, our co-created final products consistently outperformed the competition in blind taste testing.

Another benefit of organizing co-creation sessions is finding brand ambassadors. The ideal scenario when recruiting participants for a co-creation session is to select partners that have the potential to become advocates for your brand. It's beneficial to retain key opinion leaders (KOL) who are in a position to influence your target market. KOL who have participated in the product development process are much more likely to become aspirational product users in the future.

Step Four: Launch

Launch follows the co-creation phase, after you have identified authentic pain points and worked through solutions with real end-users. It is important to note that when using a lean process, you may decide to initially reduce the scale of your launch to continue the learning process. Often, brands will select a city or geographic region to launch a "beta" version before releasing a final version to the general public.

Seeing Lean Brand Building in Action

Zara

Zara uses a lean development process to quickly bring new products to market in a matter of weeks.

Ranked twenty-fifth by Interbrand Brand Rankings, Zara is considered to be one of the world's most valuable brands. With more than 2,200 stores in more than ninety countries, much of Zara's international success is rooted in a lean development process. This process enables Zara to launch on-trend clothing that has been adapted to meet local needs in only a matter of weeks.[17]

Discovery

Walk into Zara's headquarters in Spain and you will find product managers and designers busily communicating with markets like China and Chile to gain a better understanding of what's selling in local markets (see Figure 4.8).[18] Prior to the big designer shows in the major fashion capitals, Zara's design teams have already scanned the trends and have a good feel for the fabrics and colors that are becoming popular. This allows them to preselect designers they want to emulate in the following seasons.[19]

Hypothesize

Based on learning and insights, Zara's design teams produce very limited quantities of their initial design ideas, sometimes only shipping three or four dresses or shirts in each style to a store to get an initial read. [20]

Co-Create

Zara's employees are trained to observe and listen to customers, helping identify consumer needs and spot trends (see Figure 4.9). Store employees provide feedback and sales data to the headquarter design teams in order to address problems quickly. Designs are altered based on feedback, and new inventory is shipped almost immediately to replenish what has been sold.

Launch

Zara has fourteen highly automated factories located in Spain where it creates unfinished component pieces that are used as the foundation for multiple final products. This approach allows Zara to react quickly while remaining efficient. "If an item looks like a winner, Zara can quickly ramp up manufacturing and get items to their stores in a matter of days."[21]

Figure 4.8. Design area in a Zara factory.
Photo credit: Xurxo Lobato/Cover/Getty Images

Figure 4.9. Customers shopping for clothes inside a Zara shop.
Photo credit: Viorel Dudau|Dreamstime

Adidas

Adidas uses a lean process to speed up its new product launches for strategic global markets.

Taking an idea from concept to store is traditionally a very long process. The industry standard is about eighteen months for launching a new shoe style, but Adidas is able to reach markets faster.[22] Company insiders say Adidas has two defined phases in its innovation process: 1) co-create and 2) launch. I have broken those phases down into the four steps of the Lean Brand Development Model.

Discovery

Adidas discovered differences in the running styles of runners from different cities. For example, in London, people often run early in the morning and late at night to get to and from work. Londoners also have to run in the rain a lot. New York City's runners, however, run longer and faster, primarily on asphalt and concrete. So global Adidas designers began traveling to cities like London and Paris to spend more time with local runners. The design teams recruited running influencers (KOL) to collaborate with them, collecting information on their running routines: how, why, where, and when they run.[23]

Hypothesis

The company's key city journey began with the launch of the AM4LDN, made specifically for Londoners. The brand then moved on to other key cities such as Paris, Los Angeles, New York, Tokyo, and Shanghai. This new way of sequentially designing shoes allows the innovation process to remain in constant beta mode, with insights gleaned from consumers used to create hypotheses for the next city launch.

Co-Create

Adidas works with running influencers in each city to test the products designed for the unique demands for the city. Its shoes are evaluated by real runners using devices that analyze every aspect of how the athletes run. Metrics include fit and function, biometric data (forces, speeds, angles, mass, ergonomics), personal preferences (materials, colors, graphics) and usage requirements for conditions like terrain and weather. Each subsequent design idea is based on prior test data, ensuring that each iteration is continuously improved.[24]

Launch

When the design is ready for launch, the shoes are produced in larger batches by high-speed, automated robots located in an Adidas state-of-the-art SPEEDFACTORY location. At the time of this writing, Adidas has two SPEEDFACTORY locations, one in the United Sates and one in Germany (see Figures 4.10 and Figure 4.11).

Figure 4.10. AM4PAR, the Adidas shoe created specifically for Paris.
Source: Adidas, used with permission

Figure 4.11. AM4LDN, the Adidas shoe created specifically for London. Source: Adidas, used with permission

Plan Your Attack

1. Discover what motivates consumers to choose between brands and identify gaps in the solutions that are available to them to solve their needs.

2. Use the Lean Brand Canvas to work your way through each brand-building block until you have crafted a well-defined product offering.

3. Build rapid prototypes with real consumers and stakeholders to validate your value proposition.

Choose Your Stance

5

"If you want to stand out from the crowd, give people a reason not to forget you."
—Richard Branson

n martial arts, fighters adapt their style by selecting a fighting stance that takes advantage of an opponent's vulnerabilities. In marketing, we call that "positioning." Brand builders select a positioning that gives consumers a clear choice versus the competition, so purchase decisions are not based only on price. It goes without saying that just being different is never enough. A strong brand positioning must be crafted and honed until it occupies a unique and meaningful space in the minds of the consumers—a space that cannot be easily replicated by the competition.

Being a Pioneer

When launching a brand into a new international market, you must first decide if you are a "colonist" that executes the existing global positioning or a "pioneer" with the freedom and audacity to reposition a brand and create something new.

Professor Mourdoukoutas from Columbia University says that the route you choose will ultimately determine how much work is ahead of you. A pioneer commits to the long haul—a journey that requires identifying authentic consumer needs and creating a positioning that satisfies those needs in a unique way. A colonist is more specialized, focusing on adaptation and execution to bring an existing global positioning to life.[1] Ultimately, as the brand's custodian, you must follow the route that builds the strongest brand by creating a positioning that provides a competitive advantage in the new market you are entering.

In the real world, however, there is a lot of gray area. Even in situations where keeping an existing brand positioning seems like the best option, you will usually still find the need to refine and build new associations that are specific to the market you are entering.

It is also true that extending a brand into a new market requires a different thought process than launching a line or brand extension into an established market. In an established market, the target audience will likely already have some awareness of your brand, so the essence of your positioning in many ways is already predetermined. Whereas in a new market, if consumers are unaware of your brand, selecting a new positioning should be on the table for consideration.

Crafting a Compelling Brand Positioning

The process of crafting a compelling brand positioning for a new market can be distilled down to five steps (see Figure 5.1).

Let's view each step initially from a macro perspective and then see how the process works as we look at some real-world examples of how global brands developed their unique space in the minds of consumers.

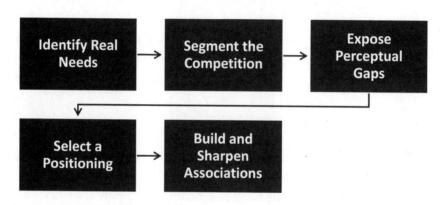

Figure 5.1. Brand positioning process.

Identify Real Needs (Functional and Emotional)

Search for real consumer needs and don't give in to the temptation to reverse engineer needs that are coincidently solved by your existing product's features and benefits. Start by putting on your consumer hat. Identify the "care-abouts" your target is attempting to satisfy and imagine your target's pain points when selecting a brand. Then utilize those identified needs to help you segment the competitive set in a meaningful way. You are ultimately looking for needs that expose a significant gap in the competitive landscape.

Remember: Your target market is unlikely to be a homogenous group of people. Some consumers will be more analytical, while others will be more conceptual. Different people process arguments and information differently. In the end, your job is to convince all of them to love your brand.

That's why the most powerful brands in the world satisfy both functional and emotional needs. Functional needs are measurable and can be solved with specific product features. Emotional needs are less tangible and have more to do with the feelings inspired by the product.

For example, let's say you are building an outdoor clothing brand. You might consider some of the following functional needs: the need to stay warm in freezing temperatures, a need for extra flexibility when climbing, or the need to stay dry in the rain. Emotional needs might include wanting to feel like a rugged and strong person, wanting to feel stylish and on-trend, or wanting to be perceived as being environmentally conscious.

In the following example, LEGO identifies an unmet need. After repositioning the brand to meet that need, LEGO's sales increased significantly.

LEGO

LEGO accelerated sales by repositioning the brand to more explicitly meet the emotional needs of children.

LEGO, the maker of those colorful, interlocking plastic bricks we all played with as children, was named the most powerful brand in 2017 by the global valuation consultancy Brand Finance.[2] However, in 2003, LEGO was on the verge of bankruptcy before it brought itself back from the brink by refreshing its brand positioning to meet both the functional and emotional needs of its target.[3]

LEGO products have always been targeted to both children and their parents. Children are the primary target while parents, as the gatekeepers, are a secondary target.

Parents have a functional need to help their children learn and harness creativity to become better problem solvers. Parents also have an emotional need to feel like they are contributing to the happiness of their offspring.

Similarly, children are functionally hardwired to play and use their imagination to build things, but they also have a strong emotional need to feel proud about their accomplishments and share their creations with their peers and family. For decades, LEGO believed that the product was king, prioritizing the functional features of its products and speaking to parents about the developmental benefits of encouraging kids to be creative.

Before repositioning, LEGO was objectively doing a suboptimal job at addressing the emotional needs of kids, especially when it came to giving children the ability to gain respect from their peers. LEGO's research revealed that kids thought the brand lacked coolness and street credibility.[4] After the repositioning, LEGO started to address kids' emotional needs head on with a new brand promise: "Joy of Building, Pride of Creation."

The Urban Dictionary defines street credibility (street cred) as "Commanding a level of respect in an urban environment due to experience in or knowledge of issues affecting those environments."[5]

Through its refreshed online communities, social media content, LEGO brand settings, and many popular entertainment collaborations, LEGO increased its street cred, giving kids more opportunities to gain respect and recognition from peers.

Segment the Competition

In their 1981 book *Positioning: The Battle for Your Mind,* Al Ries and Jack Trout wrote, "You position the product in the mind of the prospect."[6] It was true then, and it's still true now. That's why, in order to segment the competition in a meaningful way, you need to find real target consumers to help you rate each key competitive brand based on its perceived ability to satisfy the real consumer needs you identified in step one. This can be done quantitatively using statistical analysis or qualitatively using focus group discussions.

After you evaluate the competition, divide the brands up into segments based on their perceived performance. Create a perceptual map by placing each brand into a separate region on the map. Perceptual maps help to visualize the "real estate" that brands already own in the minds of target consumers and make it easier to identify and communicate positioning opportunities.

An actionable map will segment the competitive set based on needs that actually motivate consumers to choose one brand over another. In the following hypothetical perceptual map, competitive cola brands are divided up based on how natural and traditional they are perceived to be by consumers (see Figure 5.2).

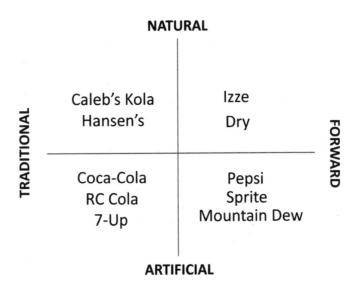

Figure 5.2. An example of a perceptual map for the United States soda market.

You should experiment using different needs to divide up the competitive landscape. Narrow down to needs that provide the most insight on opportunities to differentiate against competitors.

Beware if all the brands you are evaluating form a diagonal line when you plot them on your map. When that happens, it means that the needs you selected are too similar and your map will not help you identify a meaningful opportunity (see Figure 5.3).

It's important to remember that just because a need is real, it doesn't mean your target audience uses that need to decide between brands. The need could indeed be real, but also be part of the generic offering that all brands are expected to provide.

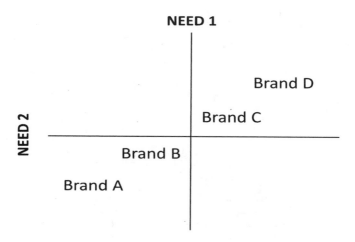

NEED 1

Brand D

Brand C

NEED 2

Brand B

Brand A

Figure 5.3. An example of overlapping attributes.

So, if all of the brands on your map stack up vertically or occupy the same quadrant, at least one of the needs that you have selected is not that important to consumers when choosing between brands (see Figures 5.4).[7]

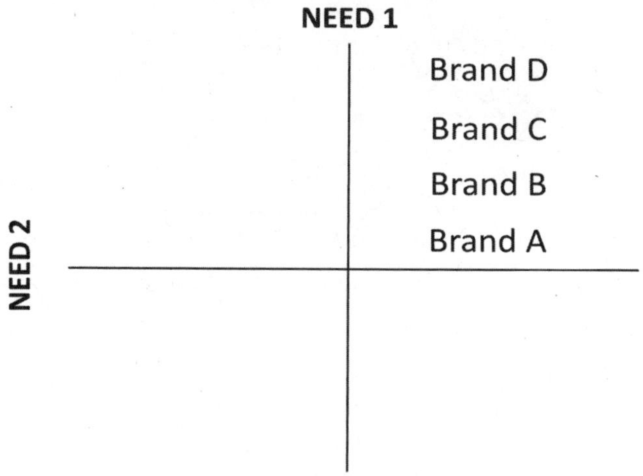

NEED 1

Brand D

Brand C

Brand B

NEED 2

Brand A

Figure 5.4. An example of an attribute that is nondifferentiating.

Expose Perceptual Gaps

Identify perceptual gaps because they represent available real estate in the minds of your consumers. Here is an analogy that has served me well: imagine that a consumer's mind is like a big city with lots of different neighborhoods that are known for specializing in different things (see Figure 5.5).

Figure 5.5. A consumer's mind is like a big city with lots of different neighborhoods.

Take New York City, for example. You have Tribeca, famous for turning commercial warehouses into luxury lofts where celebrities like Jay Z, Taylor Swift, and Robert De Niro live. South of Tribeca is the Financial District where the New York Stock Exchange and the Federal Reserve Bank are located. To the north of the Financial District are ethnic neighborhoods like Little Italy and Chinatown, which are filled with small souvenir shops and authentic eateries. So where would you live in NYC? That would depend on your needs, your personal values, and your available resources.

Look at the perceptual map you created and see if you can identify any vacant areas. Are there locations where only a few brands live today? If so, ask why. For every quadrant on your map, determine which brands are the strongest in terms of branding and market share and which are the weakest.

Select a Positioning

Now it is time to select the best location to build your brand in the minds of consumers. Select a compelling positioning that can support a differentiated and meaningful value proposition. Build a positioning in a place that allows your brand to leverage its strengths and minimize weaknesses. The ideal brand positioning also makes it hard for your competition to copy you due to their inherent strengths and weaknesses. Finally, think about how the perceptual neighborhood is evolving. Are there segments/neighborhoods where property values are increasing? What areas are in decline?

Build and Sharpen Brand Associations

Sharpen your brand's positioning by building associations that help reinforce a differentiated place in the mind of your target consumer. Use the following framework to help you calibrate associations so they strengthen your positioning and provide reassurance to consumers that your brand can deliver on its promise (see Figure 5.6).

Intentionally design associations so they amplify your brand's positive points of difference and diminish potential weaknesses. You should also try to nurture associations that help shape how your target market views the competition—associations that diminish competitive strengths and amplify competitive weaknesses.

In the following example, Levi's Japan repositioned its iconic brand to better meet the emotional needs that influence target consumers when they are deciding between brands. Levi's strengthened its positioning by building brand associations that amplified its unique claim to authenticity, thereby making it more difficult for other Japanese competitors to imitate it.

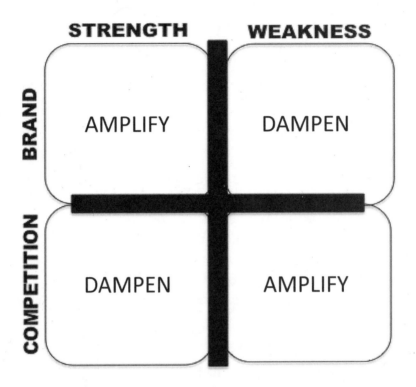

Figure 5.6. Brand association framework.

Levi's Japan

Levi's repositioned its brand for the Japan market by focusing on premium authenticity and amplifying associations related to its unique American heritage.

Global Background

From its inception in 1873, Levi's have been the every man's jean. Designed as workwear, Levi's jeans were originally called waist-overalls and constructed from denim fabric and reinforced with metal rivets.[8]

Over time, Levi Strauss & Co. started to add more styles for women, children, and teenagers (see Figure 5.7). By the 1960s, Levi's had become a ubiquitous part of Americana. To continue growing in the United States, the brand's communication began placing more emphasis on attitude and style, while de-prioritizing functionality and authenticity. When other denim brands entered the American market, they staked out areas that were not as strongly associated with the Levi's brand (see Figure 5.8).

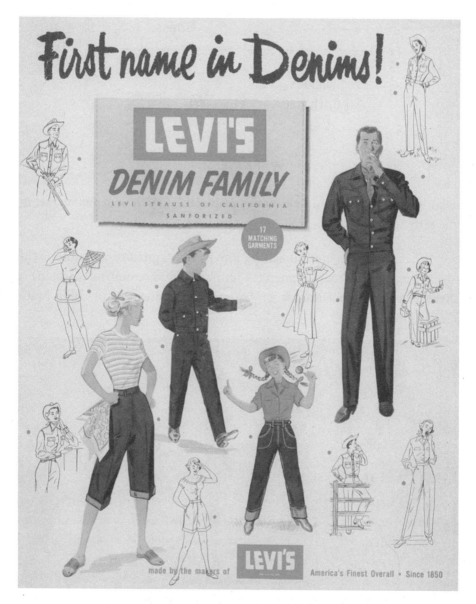

Figure 5.7. Levi's vintage poster. Source: Levi Strauss & Co. Archives (San Francisco)

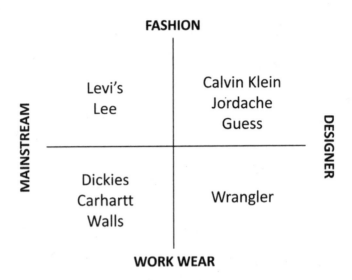

Figure 5.8. An example of a perceptual map of the American denim market in the early 1990s.

When Levi's decided to sell its low-priced Signature jean line exclusively through Walmart (America's number-one discount retail chain) in 2002, it sealed its positioning in America as a mainstream fashion brand (see Figure 5.9).

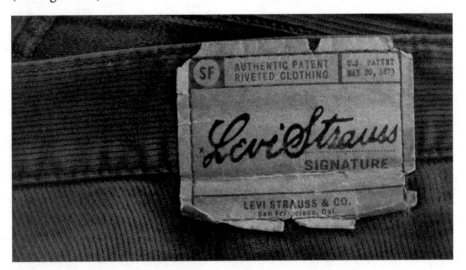

Figure 5.9. A label from Levi's Signature pants sold in Walmart.
Photo credit: iStock.com/Kislev

Being "authentically" American was no longer central to Levi's brand identity. In 2004, Levi's moved its production offshore, which resulted in its jeans no longer being manufactured in the United Sates.

Local Background

The denim market in Japan began in earnest after World War II, when Japanese youth became more exposed to American soldiers, Hollywood movies, and American fashion. Japanese culture has always valued authenticity and attention to detail. Many Japanese consumers coveted the rugged, vintage Levi's made in the United States. In fact, it wasn't uncommon for Japanese collectors in the 1980s and 1990s to travel all the way to the United States in search of vintage Levi's that would sell for as much as $3,000 a pair back in Japan.[9]

In 1982, when Levi's established an independent operating company in Japan, local Japanese brands were already selling replicas of jeans they claimed were made the way Levi's crafted their jeans back in the 1940s, 1950s, and 1960s, using vintage-style fabric, hardware, and sewing techniques. The Japanese competitive set also included other brands that prioritized meeting different consumer needs such as being on-trend or affordability.

Identify Real Needs

Culturally, Japanese consumers value attention to detail and quality craftsmanship. As a result, a large segment of the Japanese denim market prioritizes authenticity over trendier offerings. These consumers often have an emotional connection with vintage American products, romanticizing a time when things were made the old-fashioned way—with attention to detail and high-quality materials. Additionally, there is a significant number of Japanese denim buyers who value premium quality products over more mainstream and value positioned offerings.

Segment the Competition

A meaningful way to divide Japanese denim brands is based on how authentic and premium the brand is perceived to be in the minds of consumers (see Figure 5.10).

Figure 5.10. An example of a perceptual map for the 1990s Japanese denim market.

Expose Perceptual Gaps

In the 1980s, many local Japanese companies were replicating traditionally made American jeans, fueling more demand for vintage-style denim. Vintage denim's popularity created an opportunity for a real American brand to offer jeans that were crafted in the original way jeans were made a century earlier.

Select a Positioning

Instead of following the global positioning, Levi's Japan repositioned the brand specifically for the Japanese market. Iconic American entertainers like James Dean, John Wayne, Marlon Brando, Steve McQueen, and Marilyn Monroe were featured prominently in its advertising to reinforce a positioning based on premium authenticity (see Figure 5.11).

Figure 5.11. Part of an exhibition of Levi's vintage denim.
Photo credit: Alain BENAINOUS/Gamma-Rapho via Getty Images

Although the company adjusted its fit to better match Japanese bodies, it stayed true to its roots by incorporating vintage American production techniques. In addition, Levi's Japan used authentic materials such as real indigo-dyed selvage denim that was woven on vintage-style shuttle looms— just like the looms that were used to make the original Levi's denim a century earlier.

Build and Sharpen Brand Associations

While Levi's in America still focused on selling modern styles for everyone in the family, Levi's Japan doubled down on authenticity, because no matter how authentic other Japanese brands claimed to be, they could never make jeans as "real" as a pair of Levi's.

The company sharpened its authentic positioning by leveraging an accepted consumer belief that Levi's should know better than anyone else how Levi's were originally crafted. The brand maximized these authentic associations by applying Japanese attention to detail when creating branded materials and in-store displays that depicted every minute detail of its vintage American designs (see Figure 5.12)

Figure 5.12. Examples of Levi's vintage details. Photo credit: Amy Hsu

Domino's Korea

Domino's created a powerful new positioning for South Korea by understanding how the category lifecycle stage affected its target consumer.

Global Background

Pizza started as an everyday food in America. In the late 19th century when Italian immigrants arrived in the United States, they brought with them their food culture. At that time in America, pizza was perceived as an inexpensive food item, usually prepared by lower-income Italian immigrant women in their home kitchens.[10] Eventually, pizza evolved into what it is today: a classic comfort food. The average person now eats roughly forty-six slices of pizza a year in the United States. In fact, one in eight Americans will eat pizza on any given day.[11] Like most comfort foods, the price of pizza in the United States remains relatively affordable.

Pizza chain sales in the United States account for roughly $44 billion in annual sales.[12] The largest chains (Pizza Hut, Papa John's, and Domino's) reached their massive size by offering consistently good tasting, inexpensive food that is prepared quickly and delivered right to your front door.

Large chains like Domino's were able to leverage their size to continuously negotiate lower ingredient costs and then invest those savings into efficient technology like faster baking ovens and larger freezers that could hold more frozen pizza cheese.

Usually when a global pizza chain expands into a new international market, the rights to use the brand are licensed to a master franchisor. Then, the franchisor becomes responsible for operations and making adaptations to the global strategy to meet the needs of local consumers.

Local Background

The three largest pizza chains in South Korea are Pizza Hut, Domino's, and Mr. Pizza. Pizza Hut was the first to officially launch in 1985, and it concentrated its efforts on dine-in restaurants, followed by Domino's and Mr. Pizza, both of which focused on delivery service in 1990. Before the large chains arrived in Seoul, the pizza category was small and primarily made up of "mom and pop" independent shops.

Korean consumers are extremely proud of their everyday, local comfort foods. For them, pizza does not fall into that category and therefore should not be eaten too often.

Pizza plays a much different role in Korean food culture than it does in America. For starters, the pizza category in South Korea did not develop the same way as it did in the United States. In South Korea, pizza began as a premium offering, and the global chains entered the Korean market at the beginning of the category lifecycle. Being a younger category meant that chains operating in South Korea were not able to enjoy the same economies of scale as their American counterparts.

To be financially viable, Korean pizza chains raised their prices. Today, a deluxe medium-size pizza from Domino's in the United States will cost you roughly $14,[13] and it is not uncommon to find takeout pizzas promoted at much lower prices (see Figure 5.13). By contrast, the same pizza from Domino's in South Korea will cost you nearly $30 (USD).

Identify Real Needs

For many Korean consumers, eating pizza is considered entertainment and usually purchased for celebratory occasions. Pizzas by design are great for sharing and fit well with how South Koreans traditionally eat in group settings, sharing dishes placed at the center of a table.

Because the price of pizza is so expensive in South Korea, consumers expect a lot in return. Many want to be entertained when buying pizzas and expect brands to constantly introduce new flavor combinations, supported by interesting ingredient stories and unique visual elements that are impressive enough to be shared with friends.

Segment the Competition

The competitive set in South Korea can be meaningfully segmented based on how premium the offering is perceived to be and how much entertainment value the pizza provides (see Figure 5.14).

Figure 5.13. An example of takeout promotions offered at Domino's.
Photo credit: photocritical/Shutterstock

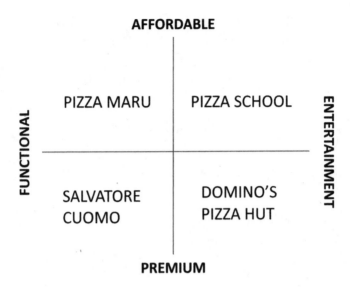

Figure 5.14. An example of a current South Korean pizza chain segmentation.

Expose Perceptual Gaps

When Domino's entered the Korean market, it identified an attractive gap in the premium-entertainment quadrant. Although there were other premium pizzas being sold, Domino's was more focused on authenticity and provenance versus entertainment.

Select a Positioning

Domino's chose a premium positioning that allowed it to increase its margins and enabled it to offer innovative pizzas made with higher-quality ingredients to appeal to those consumers who were seeking a more entertaining and special experience.

Domino's in Korea is known for its "flamboyant" pizzas.[14] The head R&D chef for Domino's Korea once told me that he tries to "shock" his consumers in order to stand out from the competition. Consequently, Domino's Korea makes some of the world's most entertaining pizzas.

The brand found success by leveraging the quality associations that come from being an American giant, while simultaneously adapting its ingredients and flavor combinations to better meet Korean consumer expectations. Some of Domino's bestselling pizza promotions from South Korea include a cheesecake pizza made with cheesecake mousse and a pizza that has a stuffed crust filled with sweet potato instead of cheese.

Build and Sharpen Associations

Domino's Korea continuously reinforces its positioning through the release of limited-time offers that shock consumers and break through the competitive clutter.

Figure 5.15. Domino's Pizza Korea launch event to promote the cheesecake sand pizza. Photo credit: The Chosunilbo JNS/Multi-Bits via Getty Images

For example, during the World Cup in Brazil, Domino's Korea launched the "Churrasco Cheese Roll Pizza," a Brazilian barbecue and pão de queijo mash-up topped with mounds of beef and vegetables encircled by rolls of cheese (see Figure 5.15).[15] Then it successfully launched a Twisted Shrimp pizza made with twisted shrimps, cherries, cookie crumbles, and cheesecake mousse. Domino's store count has been steadily growing every year over the past decade (2008–2017) to where it has now become South Korea's largest pizza chain.[16]

Coca-Cola/Minute Maid China

Coca-Cola adapted the Minute Maid global positioning to better meet the needs and constraints of the China market.

Global Background

Minute Maid launched in the United States back in the 1940s and was later acquired by Coca-Cola in 1960. A major factor in Minute Maid's success was its ability to produce frozen juice concentrate, which was a disruptive innovation at the time, making it possible for Americans to drink "real" tasting orange juice all year long (see Figure 5.16).[17]

Figure 5.16. Illustration from a vintage Minute Maid print ad.
Photo credit: Rick Thompson

Previously, the only alternative to freshly squeezed orange juice was beverage powders that didn't taste very good. In the following decades, Minute Maid became closely associated with the goodness of real orange juice, targeting its communication to families with children (see Figures 5.17 and 5.18).

Figure 5.17. 1989 Minute Maid orange juice ad. Photo credit: Rick Thompson

Figure 5.18. Vintage Minute Maid newspaper advertisement.
Photo credit: Rick Thompson

Local Background

In 2004, Coca-Cola China observed how noncarbonated drinks were growing in popularity faster than carbonated beverages. Consumers in China, like everywhere else in the world, were becoming increasingly concerned about their health and starting to pay closer attention to the ingredients in the foods, especially as more Chinese food scandals surfaced.

Unfortunately, healthy Ready-to-Drink (RTD) beverages like bottled fruit juice were not widely distributed in China due to their higher price points. The spending power of Chinese consumers in 2003 was less than one-third of what it is today.[18]

Identify Real Needs

At the time, many Chinese consumers preferred Western branded or Western looking consumer packaged goods, especially if the products were targeted to children. This was due to a belief that foreign products were made with safer ingredients. Even though retail prices were still prohibitively high for the mass market, Chinese consumers were beginning to prefer healthier beverage options like bottled juice over carbonated drinks such as cola.

Segment the Competition

The competitive set in China could be meaningfully segmented based on how foreign and healthy an offering was perceived to be in the minds of consumers (see Figure 5.19).

Expose Perceptual Gaps

Coca-Cola found that a significant opportunity existed for a reasonably priced offering, which could also be positioned as healthier than the existing RTD beverages in the market. It accurately predicted that this gap would become larger as more consumers entered the middle class.

Figure 5.19. An example of a perceptual map for the Chinese Ready-to-Drink beverage category.

Select a Positioning

Minute Maid kept true to its global brand equity regarding the goodness of juice. Minute Maid's Chinese name translates into "good juice source," which helped position the brand as a healthier beverage offering. However, for the China market, Coca-Cola chose to focus less on families and target urban Millennials instead.

In China, Minute Maid did not make a "100 percent juice" claim on its flagship product as it does in most other markets around the world (see Figure 5.20). Instead, China's Minute Maid Pulpy only contains 10 percent fruit juice. This important adaptation allowed the brand to reduce ingredient costs and become competitive with the locally manufactured juice drinks and carbonated beverages that target the growing younger middle class (see Figure 5.21).

By adding the sub-brand Pulpy, Minute Maid established a brand architecture that would give it the flexibility to add additional product lines focused on different juice-related features and benefits in the future.

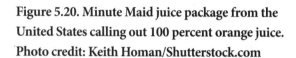

Figure 5.20. Minute Maid juice package from the United States calling out 100 percent orange juice. Photo credit: Keith Homan/Shutterstock.com

Figure 5.21. Minute Maid advert from China targeting Millennials. Source: Coca-Cola, used with permission

Build and Sharpen Associations

Minute Maid was able to create a distinctive value proposition by adding real orange pulp "Pulpy" to their drink. This unique feature not only added a more natural texture but also provided a stronger reason to believe that the drink was healthier and made with real juice.[19] Minute Maid Pulpy became the first billion-dollar Coke brand to emerge from China.[20]

L'Oreal India

L'Oréal amplified attributes of the Total Repair global brand positioning to strengthen the perception that it could meet the local needs of women in India.

Global Background

The Total Repair 5 sub-brand was originally created for the Brazilian market and launched by L'Oréal in Brazil under the Elvive brand in 2008.

Damaged hair is a big concern for many Brazilian women. According to L'Oréal's research, more than half of Brazilian women have very curly, long, dry hair. The number-one hair need for women is to repair hair that has been damaged by the sun, humidity, frequent washings, and repeated smoothing and straightening treatments.[21]

As a result, the original positioning of the Total Repair brand in Brazil was focused on hair repair. L'Oréal launched Total Repair as a range of products designed to repair the five signs of damaged hair: damaged, thinning, dullness, brittleness, and split ends (see Figure 5.22).

Figure 5.22. Elvive Total Repair line.
Photo credit: Chris Ratcliffe/Bloomberg via Getty Images

Local Background

Hair care has traditionally been a high priority for Indian women due to the importance that Indian culture places on hair appearance. L'Oréal marketers found that Indian women favor thick, long, shiny, black hair. They also want their hair to be soft and smooth.[22] Indian women had long been accustomed to buying multiple hair care products, such as an oil for dryness, conditioner for split ends, and shampoo for thinning hair.

Identify Real Needs

With 80 percent of Indian women having shoulder-length hair, L'Oréal's research found that hair care was even more important than skin care for Indian women. Traditional Indian hair rituals were often perceived to be too time consuming for modern working women. For example, L'Oréal found that a significant segment of the population felt forced into using multiple hair products just to keep their hair manageable. To prevent hair from breaking, falling out, and becoming dull, women would shampoo, oil, and condition every time they washed their hair.[23]

Segment the Competition

The competitive set for the shampoo market in India could be meaningfully segmented based on how premium a brand was perceived to be and how many hair care benefits it provided (see Figure 5.23).

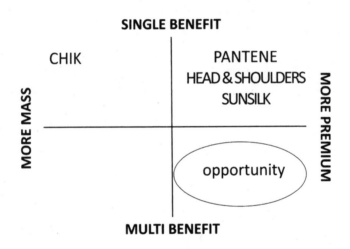

Figure 5.23. An example of the Indian shampoo market.

Expose Perceptual Gaps

The L'Oréal marketing team found a gap in the premium/multibenefit segment of the market. While other premium offerings like Pantene focused on singular benefits like emphasizing shine, or Head & Shoulders, which promoted itself as a solution for dandruff, there weren't any premium-positioned products that promised to provide an all-in-one solution for a woman's many hair care needs.

Select a Positioning

L'Oréal took the Total Repair 5 brand from Brazil and launched it under the L'Oréal brand in India as a premium-priced offering on par with Procter & Gamble's Head & Shoulders. In India, L'Oréal already had a strong reputation in hair care. The company leveraged the success of its L'Oréal Excellence Hair Color line to gain shelf space and additional distribution for the Total Repair offering.

Total Repair 5 was launched into the Indian market promising women a total solution for all their hair needs: hair shedding, dry hair, rough hair, dull hair, and split ends.

Build and Sharpen Associations

L'Oréal sharpened its positioning by explicitly calling out how Total Repair 5 contains a proprietary ingredient named Ceramide-Cement that makes hair strong, supple, smooth, shiny, and protects tips. L'Oréal then amplified Total Repair's associations with beautiful, healthy hair by hiring Aishwarya Rai, a famous Indian model and actress known for her gorgeous hair, to become the brand's spokesperson (see Figure 5.24). As a result, L'Oréal's efforts in India have helped grow the category. L'Oréal is now on track in India to become a $1 billion brand by 2020.[24]

Figure 5.24. Aishwarya Rai, L'Oréal spokesperson.
Photo credit: Andrea Raffin/Shutterstock

Mizone

Danone repositioned the Mizone brand to appeal to the needs of a larger target market in China.

Global Background

Mizone was originally launched in New Zealand as a sports drink, targeting people who play active sports. Deeply rooted in British colonial heritage, New Zealand has a long-established organized sports culture. For example, 33 percent of young people and 20 percent of adults in New Zealand are involved with sports clubs, and almost all men (90 percent) watch sports on television.[25]

Mizone was less sweet than Gatorade, the global sport drink leader at the time, and was made from purified water and natural fruit flavors. The brand's communication and activities were focused on individual athletes engaging in exhausting physical activity such as running and playing football (see Figure 5.25).

Figure 5.25. An athlete competing in the 2998km Mizone New Zealand Endurazone race. Photo credit: Ross Land/Getty

Local Background

In China, participation in organized sports is not as popular as it is in New Zealand. Mothers in China generally prefer their children to study instead of playing sports. Even in a tier-one city like Shanghai, the percentage of youth participating in organized sports is only half of what it is in New Zealand.[26]

However, while the majority of China's youth may not compete in organized sports, they do face fierce competition in school, at work, and in their social lives. With a population of nearly 1.4 billion, just getting into a top-rated university is extremely competitive, and it doesn't end there. The unemployment rate is roughly three times higher for recent graduates versus the general population in China.[27] This is because each year, six million new graduates enter the workforce, plus another three million migrant workers arrive in the big cites looking for a better way of life.[28]

For Chinese men, even dating has become incredibly competitive. A remnant from the country's one child policy is that there is still a serious shortage of marrying-age women in China. On average, only 100 girls are born for every 118 boys.[29] By 2020, it is estimated that there will be thirty million more Chinese men than women looking for someone to marry.[30]

Identify Needs

Because of the numerous food safety scandals that were widely covered in the news, a growing number of Chinese consumers began expressing more interest in food products manufactured by brands from developed countries. Along with being more concerned about food safety, consumers wanted products made from real ingredients. Chinese consumers have always paid close attention to the ingredients in their food, as many common foods are known to have functional benefits based on traditional Chinese medicine.

Finally, many younger Chinese consumers desired products that could help them replenish their strength and provide an advantage during life's many stressful activities beyond playing sports.

Segment the Competition

When analyzing the China market, the competitive set can be segmented based on the type of physical activity a drink is designed to supplement and whether the brand is perceived as being of local or foreign origin (see Figure 5.26).

Figure 5.26. An example of a perceptual map for performance drinks in China.

Expose Perceptual Gaps

A meaningful gap was found in the everyday performance/foreign brand quadrant. Even though Quaker Oats had introduced Gatorade into China in 1995, the brand was still extremely underdeveloped and focused primarily on athletic performance. There was also a popular local sports drink named Jianlibao that was known for sponsoring local Chinese athletes.

In the past, when average Chinese consumers wanted a drink to help quench their thirst or replenish fluids after strenuous activity, they would usually turn to traditional-style drinks like green tea and grass jelly.

Select a Positioning

Danone, the owner of the Mizone brand, positioned Mizone in China as a flavored water drink fortified with vitamins and minerals, designed to support Millennials as they perform life's important activities like going to school, working, and spending time with friends. This significant shift from the original positioning in New Zealand enabled Mizone to target a much larger market in China.

Mizone China advertisements depicted groups of friends having fun, and interacting with colleagues and classmates (see Figure 5.27).

Figure 5.27. Mizone China advertisement. Source: Danone, with permission

Sharpen and Build Associations

Mizone sharpened their positioning by leveraging the insight that everyday life was extremely competitive for young people living in China. Younger Chinese have very little personal free time to socialize outside of work. So when they do find time to do something with their friends, they want to have enough strength and mental clarity to enjoy that time together. This was an authentic consumer need that Mizone associated itself with through its brand communication. The brand continued to amplify this association through a battle cry that eventually evolved into "Mizone restores you to the ideal state at any time."

Plan Your Attack

1. Identify the real needs your target is attempting to satisfy when choosing a brand.

2. Segment the competitors based on those needs to expose a perceptual gap in the competitive set.

3. Sharpen and build associations that strengthen your positioning and make it difficult for your competitors to follow.

Adapt to Win 6

"You must be shapeless, formless, like water. When you pour water in a cup, it becomes the cup. When you pour water in a bottle, it becomes the bottle. When you pour water in a teapot, it becomes the teapot. Water can drip and it can crash. Become like water my friend."

–Bruce Lee

"It is not the strongest of the species that survives, nor the most intelligent; it is the one most adaptable to change."

–Charles Darwin

When I first started in brand management there was an ongoing debate about whether or not Western brands could succeed by focusing on exporting their standard products into developing markets with little to no adaptation. In the early 2000s, there wasn't a strong need to adapt because when most Western brands expanded into developing markets, they didn't face serious competition in terms of quality. The situation has changed. Local brands continue to improve and develop new products specifically tailored to meet the needs of emerging consumers. Today, aspiring global brands must accept what they had long tried to ignore: global brands do need to adapt to win in local markets.

Getting Better All the Time

As a child, I remember when Japan had a reputation for making inexpensive toys, knockoffs, and trinkets that many Americans classified as "cheap" in both price and quality. With Japan's embrace of Dr. Deming's statistical quality control and the rise of titans like Sony, Nissan, Honda, and Toyota, those perceptions faded. It wasn't long after that when Japanese brands became synonymous with high quality.

As a teenager, I remember having a similar attitude toward products made in Korea. A high school friend of mine owned an early model Kia that was inexpensive, noisy, and didn't brake well. I can recall buying a Goldstar VHS player from Costco because I couldn't afford a higher quality, more expensive Sony model. As an adult, I find the quality of Korean products is revered around the world: LG (Lucky-Goldstar) became famous for its paper-thin television screens; Kia and Hyundai make some of the safest and bestselling cars in the world, and Samsung is now the world's second largest phone manufacturer after Apple.

No longer can developed market brands simply assume they will have an advantage when it comes to quality. Even if a developed market brand manages to create a quality advantage, it will only be a matter of time until a developing market brand catches up, proving that the necessity for building strong brands has never been more important. Brands are what separate commodities from higher margin premium-priced products. A global survey conducted by Nielsen found that 38 percent of all respondents believe a product produced by a well-known or trusted brand makes the product more "premium."[1]

Think Global, Act Local

With more global marketers in agreement that one size does not fit all, the term "GLOCAL" (Think Global, Act Local) has been getting a lot more use in marketing circles. According to the American Marketing Association, "The term GLOCAL has been coined to describe an organizational approach that provides clear global strategic direction along with the flexibility to adapt to local opportunities and requirements."[2]

Nike CEO Mike Parker recently announced that the company would begin to develop what he called a "local business, on a global scale" and "deeply" serve customers in a dozen key cities, including New York, Paris, Beijing, and Milan. These twelve mega-cities are expected to deliver 80 percent of Nike's growth during the next two and a half years.[3]

A global survey conducted by Millward Brown across eight countries revealed that although global brands tend to be stronger than local brands overall, local brands generally score higher on being part of a national culture, which research shows is a major driver of purchase intent.[4]

What Should You Adapt?

Experience has taught me that when a global brand is planning to enter an international market, the million-dollar question is: What parts of the existing value proposition need to be adapted and which parts should remain consistent with the global strategy?

When trying to decide what to adapt, it's helpful to drill down to the attributes that will most likely influence consumers as they make their purchasing decision. That's why I developed the following framework for helping my teams zoom in on categories of brand associations that most influence the purchase of a foreign brand (see Figure 6.1).

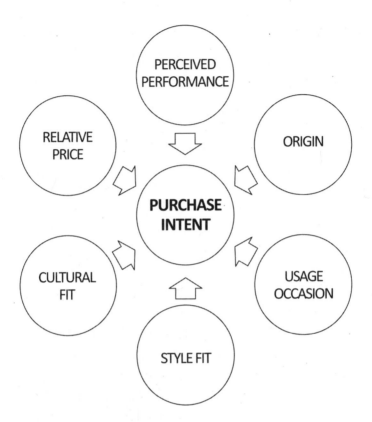

Figure 6.1. Categories of brand associations that influence the purchase intent for foreign brands.

In reality, all of these factors are highly correlated, so it's the thought process that is important to master. Feel free to add or subtract associations that you believe are more relevant to the product category you are entering. Remember: The weighting of associations is highly dependent on the product category, target market, and competitive environment.

The Evaluation Process

To gain clarity on which parts of the value proposition need to be adapted, evaluate your brand on each of the six categories of associations that tend to influence the purchase intent for foreign brands. Do this to determine whether or not a category represents an area of strength or weakness for your brand versus competitors. If the category is a strength, ask what adaptations can be made to make the associations stronger. If the category is a weakness, ask what adaptations can be made to make the associations become more advantageous for your brand.

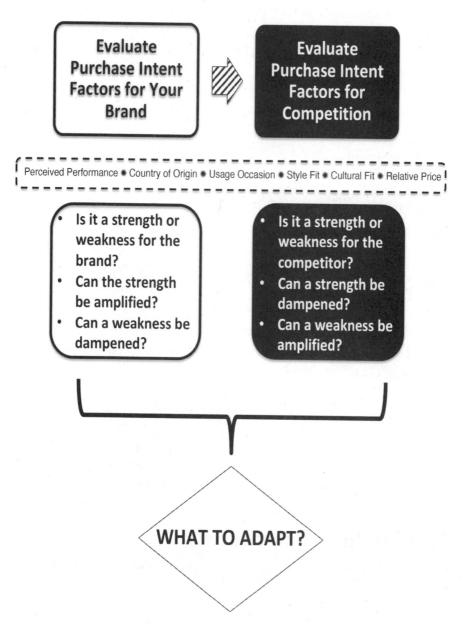

Figure 6.2. Global brand adaptation framework.

Then, evaluate your key competitor on *each* of the *same* six categories versus your brand. Just as you did with your brand, assess if a category represents an area of strength or weakness, but this time judge from the perspective of the competitor. If the category is perceived to be a strength for your competitor, look for associations that you can add to your brand that would make consumers perceive that area to be less strong for your competitor. Similarly, if the category is perceived to be a weakness for the competitor, try to identify associations that can be added to your brand to take advantage of the perceived weakness (see Figure 6.2 on page 111).

The following section discusses each category of associations in more detail using select case studies to bring the evaluation process to life.

Perceived Performance

Many marketers believe that a product's "actual" performance is where the "rubber meets the road," but Al Ries believes "perceived" performance is actually more important. In his AdAge article, "Having a Better Brand Is Better Than Having a Better Product," Ries argues that there ". . . are no superior products. There are only superior perceptions in consumers' minds."[5]

I admit that's a provocative statement, but one with a lot of truth to it. This is because the technical differences between leading brands are usually very small. Compare the performance reviews for leading mobile phones and you will see just how true this is.

To use an American football analogy, I am a firm believer that product performance needs to get you into the red zone (the area of the field between the 20-yard line and the goal line). After which, it is up to the brand equity you have created to get you over the goal line. Don't get me wrong. If there is a product gap, by all means close it. Your main objective is to always strive to be better than the competition, but don't forget that your competition is doing the same thing. Inevitably, you will have to accept that from time to time your actual product advantage may be negligible.

During my tenure at Nestlé's global policy was not to launch a new product unless it scored at least a 60 percent preference versus the competition in blind taste testing. If you're wondering why the bar was set at only 60 percent, it turns out it is very hard to develop new products that taste better than that of leading competitors. The best brands in the world are all simultaneously investing R&D resources into discovering new ways to exceed consumer expectations through renovation and innovation.

So why do consumers have very specific brand preferences when so many branded products are actually the same from a technical perspective? At the end of the day, it boils down to the power of the brand. Perceived performance is only the "perception" or "estimate" of a brand's actual quality in the minds of consumers.

This means, in order to elevate perceived performance in the minds of consumers you can and should always try to create brand associations that generate positive performance perceptions.

Amplifying and Dampening Brand Associations

The following examples examine ways in which some brands have strengthened their perceived performance by amplifying and dampening brand associations.

"Birds of a feather flock together" makes sense, right? As you might expect, research supports that people are attracted to others who hold similar views and express similar attitudes, and the attraction increases with the more they have in common.[6] A study using behavioral data collected from Facebook "likes" and status updates confirms that "people date and befriend others who are like themselves."[7] This is really good news for brand builders. Since consumers intuitively believe birds of a feather do indeed flock together, you can borrow brand associations from other brands that have stronger perceived performance by simply placing your brand in close proximity.

We all know instinctively that a retailer's store environment and image affect how consumers view the products sold in that store. There is research that takes this further by suggesting that when a low-image brand is placed in a high-image retailer, consumer perceptions regarding the low-image brand significantly increase.[8] That is why new fashion designers will do almost anything for the opportunity to get their brands carried by a specialty retailer like Barneys New York.

Barneys New York

Barneys is a high-end specialty department store with twenty-four shops located in the United States and twelve licensed shops in Japan. According to Executive Chairman Mark Lee, Barneys tries to offer the most beautiful and best products in the world.[9] The CEO of Barneys, Daniella Vitale, says her team "is committed to securing exclusive product and developing emerging brands at every price point."[10]

Barneys has received a lot of attention for its exclusive artist and designer collaborations. Jay Z, Russell Westbrook, and Justin Bieber are just some of the celebrities and artists who have created items exclusively for Barneys (see Figures 6.3 and 6.4).

Consumers believe that if a brand is carried by Barneys, it must be prestigious. The brands selected benefit from the consumer perception that the specialty retailer only carries high-quality brands.

Figure 6.3. Justin Bieber's collaboration with Barneys.
Photo credit: James Devaney/Getty. Images for Barneys New York

Figure 6.4. Jay Z's "A New York Holiday" gift bags at Barneys.
Source: Sagmeister & Walsh

It is not always possible to get listed into a retailer like Barneys to amplify your brand's performance perceptions. However, there are many other things that you can do to augment the way your brand is presented to the consumer.

When entering a new market, the performance perception of your brand may be low because consumers are unfamiliar with the brand. In this case, you can use in-store point-of-sale (POS) materials, product displays, and sampling to amplify perceptions and shape how consumers view your brand.

Innisfree

Innisfree is a very popular Korean cosmetics company with more than four hundred locations in South Korea alone. The brand focuses on skin care and promises consumers healthier looking skin when consumers use its natural products. Innisfree relies on the origin of its ingredients as a primary reason to believe in the brand's promise. The ingredients are sourced from Jeju Island in South Korea, which is known for its "clear fresh air, soft warm sunlight, fertile healthy soil and pure water."[11]

While the majority of South Korean's are very familiar with the wonders of Jeju Island, foreign consumers need to be educated about the island and all the benefits that come from these pure ingredients.

Suh Kyung-Bae, the company's chairman and CEO says, "Whenever we go into a new country, we need to first understand what our customers like and how best to communicate the brand story."[12] When Innisfree builds a new store in an international market, the company creates highly visual, interactive displays that bring the Korean brand story to life. Since Innisfree can't assume foreign consumers will know about Jeju Island, it goes to great lengths to describe the origin of ingredients and the various features of the popular Korean island (see Figures 6.5 and 6.6).

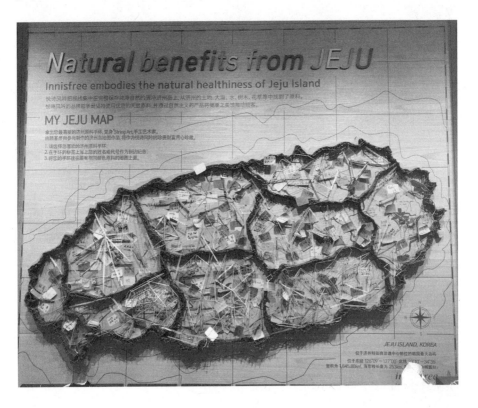

Figure 6.5. Innisfree store display in Shanghai highlighting different areas of Jeju Island, Korea. Photo credit: Amy Hsu

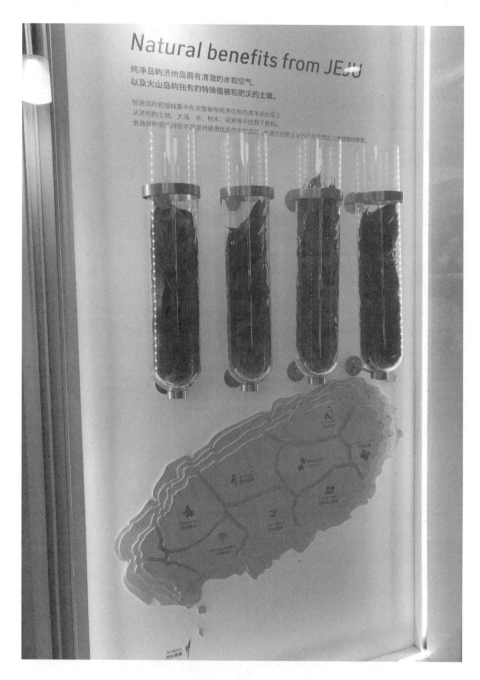

Figure 6.6. Innisfree China in-store display educating consumers about Jeju Island, Korea. Photo credit: Amy Hsu

Sunny Hills

Sunny Hills is a premium positioned bakery concept that uses a romantic ingredient story to support its high-quality offering. Sunny Hills launched in Taiwan and is now expanding throughout Asia with locations in Singapore, Japan, and Mainland China.

If you are not from Taiwan, then you are probably not aware of how Sunny Hills uses delicious pineapples grown in "the sunny and rugged countryside of Bagua Mountain in central Taiwan."[13] Bagua is famous for its tea, pineapples, and a big statue of Buddha.

Sunny Hills uses an engaging sampling ritual to help elevate quality perceptions. Upon entering a store, customers are offered a "complimentary piece of pineapple cake, with a light, flaky crust and a gooey pineapple jam filling, accompanied by a cup of oolong tea."[14] Then, a brand advocate will tell interested customers about how the pineapple cakes taste the way they do because of the delicious pineapples sourced from Bagua Mountain (see Figure 6.7).

Figure 6.7. Sunny Hills in-store ritual sample of pineapple cake and tea.
Photo credit: Amy Hsu

Nespresso

I recently received a delicious sample cup of Nespresso coffee made from single origin coffee beans while browsing in a shopping mall in Shanghai. These days, I've been noticing many more Nespresso boutiques, with their modern and sophisticated décor, intentionally located in high-end shopping malls throughout Asia (see Figure 6.8).

Figure 6.8. Nespresso Boutique, Taiwan. Photo credit: Amy Hsu

Nestlé, a company not really known for its cool factor, has positioned the Nespresso brand in China as part of a sophisticated lifestyle.[15] Nespresso has become an aspirational brand in China, representing one of the fastest growing markets for the brand globally.

For years, as I traveled throughout the Asia region, I noticed stylish, little Nespresso machines strategically placed in trendy, aspirational locations like five-star hotels, creative agencies, and luxury fashion boutiques (see Figure 6.9).

Figure 6.9. Hotel room Nespresso machine. Photo credit: Amy Hsu

Alfonso Troisi, the country manager of Nespresso China, says Chinese consumers want "a full shopping experience" and most of them spend a minimum of thirty minutes at Nespresso's boutique stores, talking to coffee specialists about their preferences and departing with their own personalized collections.[16] Through its boutiques and by partnering with trendy, high-end establishments and brands, Nespresso is building positive perceptions regarding quality and performance, while also linking the brand closely with a modern, sophisticated lifestyle.

Brand Alliances

Creating brand alliances gives you an opportunity to borrow positive associations from other brands. There is a lot of flexibility when it comes to creating brand alliances because connections can be formed in multiple ways, as illustrated in the following examples.

Huawei

China's Huawei is the world's largest telecommunications equipment manufacturer and third largest smartphone brand in the world. Richard Yu, the company's CEO, publicly stated that his goal for the brand is to become the second-largest smartphone brand.[17]

Huawei's technology is very competitive by all accounts. However, research conducted in Western Europe found that Huawei's brand image, when compared to Apple and Samsung, was negatively affected by a country-of-origin bias with regards to product quality.[18] In 2017, Huawei's YouGov BrandIndex Impression score, a measurement of how positive consumers are feeling about a brand, scored Huawei around the (+4) mark,[19] compared to brands like Apple iPhone and Samsung that scored considerably higher at roughly (+28).[20]

Huawei has built several brand alliances to help combat this perception and elevate quality perceptions internationally. It recently launched a line of mobile phones that are cobranded with the Leica brand (see Figure 6.10).

Figure 6.10. Huawei coengineered with Leica in-store signage.
Photo credit: Amy Hsu

Leica is an internationally operating, premium-segment manufacturer of cameras and sport optics products. The Leica brand has a very high-quality image that traces back to 1925 in Germany, and cobranding provides a strong reason for consumers to believe in Huawei's high performance (see Figure 6.11).[21]

Huawei also sells a cobranded Porsche design phone and makes use of various sponsorships and celebrity endorsements to help elevate performance perceptions. For example, the brand sponsors several high-performing football teams across Europe including Arsenal, Borussia Dortmund, and Ajax Amsterdam. To launch its new flagship smartphones in the West, Scarlett Johansson and Henry Cavill, who both play superheroes on screen, were hired to boost awareness and performance perceptions (see Figure 6.12).

Figure 6.11. Huawei in-store advertisement featuring Leica brand alliance. Photo credit: Amy Hsu

Figure 6.12. Huawei billboard advertisement featuring Scarlett Johansson and Henry Cavill. Photo credit: istanbulphotos/Shutterstock

Semiotics

If you want to increase the perceived performance of your brand in the minds of consumers, consider fine-tuning your brand's use of semiotics. Marketing semiotics is the study of how consumers interpret design, language, visuals, and even sound to make sense of a brand's positioning and value offering.

According to Laura Oswald, author of *Creating Value, the Theory and Practice of Marketing Semiotics Research,* each product category has a defined semiotic code.[22] These symbolic codes vary by market and are formed in the minds of consumers over time as a result of brands using common symbols in their advertising, packaging, and communication materials. For example, in most markets, a picture of a heart tells consumers that a product is heart-healthy, a cartoon mascot indicates that a product is for kids, and the color black usually indicates a premium positioning. Brand builders can take advantage of how consumers rely on semiotic codes to provide a shortcut for understanding products, and intentionally reinforce a desired brand positioning and value proposition.

Coca-Cola

In China, there are an estimated 335 million teenagers, and Coca-Cola would like them all to fall in love with the Coke brand. Unfortunately for Coke, there is a lot of competition, with roughly one thousand ready-to-drink beverage options vying for the attention of China's prized younger consumers.

Today, Coke is facing a global problem because it's losing the battle with younger consumers who represent the future of the brand. Younger consumers are increasingly opting for drinks like noncarbonated teas, water, or juice that seem healthier. As a result, Classic Coke's market share is declining globally, and the brand is now under-indexing in the very important eighteen to twenty-four age group.[23]

Coca-Cola China recently launched thirty-five limited edition Coke labels designed to resonate with Chinese teenagers by speaking to them in their own youth language (see Figure 6.13).

The new labels were co-created with McCann Worldgroup and contain a mixture of emoticons, numbers, characters, and graphics representing authentic "code" that Millennials use to text phrases like "I love you" and "Good luck."

Shelly Lin, Coke's marketing director for China, explained, "Nowadays in China, teens are using modern communication that is more than language and they have created a lot of new ways to express themselves. We thought that we can build a meaningful conversation with millennials by speaking their language, instead of just borrowing icons that are already there."[24]

Coca-Cola China is also using teenage celebrity endorsers, such as pop star sensation Lu Han, to promote its new bottles and engage with his more than forty million Weibo social media followers (see Figure 6.14).[25]

Figure 6.13. Coca-Cola China's limited-edition "code" packaging targeted at younger consumers. Source: Coca-Cola, used with permission

Figure 6.14. Coca-Cola China promotional materials featuring Lu Han.
Photo credit: Amy Hsu

Word of Mouth

According to a study conducted by McKinsey & Company, word of mouth plays a larger role in the decision-making process of emerging-market consumers than it does in developed markets. This is mainly due to "the higher mix of first-time buyers, a shorter history with the brand, a culture of societal validation, and a fragmented media landscape."[26] First-time buyers in a market where a brand is not well-known need extra assurances that the brand in question will perform as promised.

Therefore, the source of information becomes very important in an emerging market where consumers trust what real people tell them more than advertising slogans from unknown companies.

Dettol China

The cleaning and disinfectant brand Dettol wanted to relaunch into tier-two Chinese cities like Nanjing where less than 10 percent of households were using the brand. The Dettol team conducted a series of ethnographies in Nanjing designed to gain a better understanding of how consumers were using the brand. What it found was that moms in Nanjing were using Dettol only for big tasks like deep cleaning and washing floors even though the product works well for many smaller everyday tasks like sanitizing hands and keeping kitchen surfaces clean.

In order to encourage consumers to use Dettol more often, the brand team hired Advocacy, a word-of-mouth agency, to recruit four thousand high-profile influencers from Nanjing who had the potential to become brand ambassadors. The group consisted of local moms who each had a large network of friends. Influencers were given ten small spray bottles of Dettol to share with their networks. The bottles were an instant hit. In fact, they were so popular that another fifty thousand bottles had to be produced immediately to satisfy demand.

Through this campaign, Dettol was able to reach 46 percent of its target consumers in Nanjing. Top-of-mind awareness for the brand increased 500 percent, and shipments for the brand rose by more than 80 percent versus the precampaign average. Advocacy claims that this campaign was fifteen times more efficient than television.[27]

Country of Origin (COO)

When launching a brand into an international market, it's important to be aware of how your brand's country of origin (COO) will be perceived by the local target consumers. When the COO is viewed as a positive, you can then look for ways to amplify the positive associations. When the COO is negative, you need to dampen that perception by augmenting the way the COO is expressed to the consumer.

Nielsen completed a global survey in 61 countries and found that nearly three-quarters of the respondents claim COO is an important factor when making a purchase decision. Furthermore, developing-market respondents were "more likely than their developed-market counterparts to say that local brands are more attuned to their personal needs/tastes," but that "global brands offer the latest product innovations and are of better quality." Nielsen found that across markets, there are some general preferences for specific product categories. For example, respondents typically preferred local COO brands when it came to food items.[28]

Wendy's Japan

Although Japanese consider hamburgers to be an American food, most will tell you that Japan has perfected the classic American fast food. For example, one of my favorite burger shops in the world is located in Tokyo at Omotesando Hills Shopping Center. The little shop is called Golden Brown, and it is known for its gourmet-style burgers made from grass-fed Australian beef and fresh buns baked with wild yeast. The store sells nearly three thousand burgers a week.[29] When I observed the guys in the kitchen at Golden Brown making their burgers, I couldn't help but feel as if I were watching artisans at work. With each ingredient prepared and placed on the burgers with careful precision, I wondered if this was the way burgers were made back in the 1950s before they became a mass-produced product (see Figure 6.15).

Figure 6.15. Golden Brown Burger, Japan.
Photo credit: metamorworks/Shutterstock

There are an estimated two thousand independent burger shops in Japan, as well as big burger chains like McDonald's, Burger King, and MOS burger (a Japanese chain).[30] All of them have menus that have been adapted to cater to the tastes of local Japanese consumers. In fact, McDonald's Japan recently decided to discontinue the classic American Quarter Pounder to make room for more Japan-friendly items like the popular Ebi Filet-O, Teriyaki McBurger, and McPork.

In 2016, Wendy's announced a relaunch of its brand into the Japanese market. As part of its relaunch strategy, Wendy's Japan acquired First Kitchen, a popular Japanese fast-casual chain with more than 130 locations throughout Japan. First Kitchen is well known for its Japanese-friendly menu and for placing a heavy emphasis on pasta and burgers. To support the relaunch, Wendy's rebranded all of the First Kitchen stores to Wendy's First Kitchen (see Figure 6.16). The new concept offers a blended menu from both Wendy's and First Kitchen's existing menus.

By cobranding with First Kitchen, Wendy's was able to dampen the negative associations of being just another American fast-food chain, and lowered the risk of trial for Japanese consumers since First Kitchen is already a trusted brand in Japan.

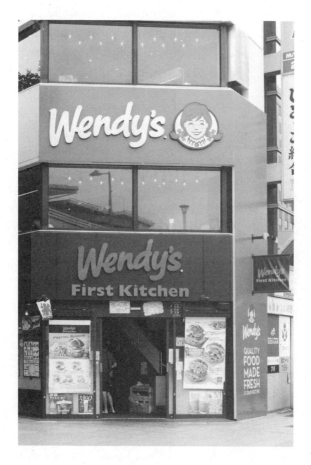

Figure 6.16. Wendy's First Kitchen, Japan.
Photo credit: Ned Snowman/Shutterstock

Beats by Dre

Beats by Dr. Dre (Beats) is a leading audio brand that was founded by the legendary Dr. Dre and Jimmy Iovine. Beats was acquired by Apple in 2014 and has consistently shown an ability to use its team of international brand ambassadors to generate word of mouth in local markets.

According to Omar Johnson, the company's CMO, the brand ambassadors or "influencers," as he calls them, play a critical role in Beats campaigns. He refers to them as the "ingredients" that build campaigns. Johnson says that the influencers "live in culture, music, sports, art and fashion, and as much as we're good communicators, our strongest muscle as a brand is our listening muscle. We listen to influencers, we talk to them and build relationships."[31]

Figure 6.17. Beats by Dre in-store poster, Shanghai. Photo credit: Amy Hsu

In 2015, Beats partnered with Universal Pictures to promote the movie *Straight Outta Compton,* which tells the story of how Dr. Dre's hip-hop group NWA rose to fame. To get consumers excited about the movie and promote Beats products, the brand activated its network of international influencers to introduce www.StraightOuttaSomewhere.com to its fans.

The site enabled visitors to create custom memes that highlighted the cities where they came from. For example, in China, Beats partnered with Kris Wu, a famous Chinese rapper and actor, to represent his hometown of Guangzhou. Beats made Kris an official spokesperson for the brand and was able to engage with his 11.7 million Weibo followers (see Figure 6.17 on page 130).[32]

The campaign was a huge success. Beats became the first brand in history to be the number-one trending topic on Facebook, Twitter, and Instagram all at the same time, with 8.7 million memes created and shared via social media.[33]

Beats continued to build on that momentum by launching the "Straight Outta Asia" campaign that encouraged regional pride by featuring a wide range of Asian influencers that included musicians, actors, artists, and media personalities (see Figures 6.18 and 6.19).[34]

In most Asian countries, China is currently perceived to have more influence than the United States. In many Asian countries there are also many Chinese consumers who now believe the United States doesn't want China to get any stronger.

A Pew Research Center survey conducted in 2015 found that "More than half (54 percent) of Chinese believed the United States was trying to prevent China from becoming as powerful as the United States. Only 28 percent said the United States accepts that China will become as powerful."[35]

Figure 6.18. A Shanghai-based singer on a Beats poster in a Shanghai shopping center. Photo credit: Amy Hsu

Figure 6.19. A Chinese model on a Beats poster in a Chinese mall.
Photo credit: Amy Hsu

Which country has most influence in Asia now?		
	China	United States
Vietnam	60%	18%
Taiwan	61%	22%
Mongolia	61%	9%
Japan	61%	27%
Singapore	54%	29%
China	58%	28%
Korea	67%	25%
Thailand	49%	19%
Malaysia	42%	46%
Cambodia	27%	46%
Indonesia	37%	37%
Philippines	22%	59%
Myanmar	57%	32%
Data source: ABS Wave IV (2014-2016)		

Figure 6.20. Countries with the strongest influence in Asia.

Helen Wang, an expert on China's middle class, says that Chinese youth are conflicted between their national pride and their love for Western brands. In Forbes, she wrote about how Victoria Secret failed at an attempt to appeal to Chinese Millennials when it used Western models to showcase its dragon-themed lingerie. Many Chinese consumers took to social media and complained how the outfits were distasteful and didn't represent real Chinese culture.[36]

There is always the risk that if not executed properly, local consumers can experience cognitive dissonance when a global brand enters a local market. By having international influencers "represent" not only Beats but also their hometowns, the Beats brand became more relevant to local consumers, and was able to dampen potential negative associations arising from an American brand promoting itself in a market like China.

Usage Occasion

Consumers need to be able to accurately gauge a product's usage occasion to evaluate the brand's value proposition. When consumers are unable to categorize the brand offering correctly, it can spell disaster, as illustrated in the following story of the launch of Trix breakfast cereal in China.

To prepare for our launch of Nestlé breakfast cereals into China in 2002, my team conducted extensive focus groups with local Chinese consumers to evaluate the existing offerings from our global portfolio. It caught us to-tally by surprise that when we showed Chinese consumers cereal packages from developed markets, most of the respondents had no idea what the intended usage occasion was or even how breakfast cereal should be eaten.

Breakfast cereal packaging from developed markets like the United Sates makes assumptions. The biggest one is that consumers already understand the category. For example, an illustration of an animal on the front of a cereal package doesn't make an American mother think of pet food. However, when we showed Chinese moms kid cereal packaging from developed markets, they thought the packages looked like dog food. In addition, most couldn't figure out how the product was supposed to be eaten (see Figure 6.21).

Figure 6.21. Trix Packaging from the United States.
Photo credit: Sheila Fitzgerald/Shutterstock

Figure 6.22. Trix back-of-pack communication from the China launch.
Photo credit: Amy Hsu

The packaging from developed markets did not need to have visual cues to help explain the product because consumers from developed markets already understand the concept of breakfast cereal. Yet, even after we explained to Chinese moms that the product was in fact a breakfast food made for kids, they initially assumed that kids should eat it dry, with their hands, the way people eat potato chips or popcorn.

Our launch addressed these issues by making sure the final packaging called out the breakfast eating occasion and contained detailed instructions on how to prepare and eat the cereal. We even made sure to print photos of Chinese children enjoying breakfast cereal with a spoon and bowl on the back of the packs (see Figure 6.22 on page 136).

Special Occasions

Using research from the wine industry, we know that consumers will pay more for a bottle of wine when it's intended for a special occasion or given as a gift.[37] Gifting, in many international markets, represents a huge sales opportunity. According to Dayalan Nayager, the managing director for Diageo Global Travel business unit, gifting represents one-third of all purchases for Diageo.[38] However, consumers must be able to see the quality of the product and understand its intended use, especially when buying premium-priced gifts and luxury goods.

One of the best ways to communicate a product's usage occasion is through packaging. Impressive packaging designs and aesthetics can communicate product quality and make consumers feel less price sensitive.[39] In a global study on Millennials, Deloitte found that "Quality and uniqueness are the most important factors drawing Millennial consumers to luxury products."[40]

Diageo commissioned award-winning Taiwanese artist Page Tsou to create four new label designs for its latest Chinese New Year Johnnie Walker Blue Label series. Tsou said, "This unique design tells the story of Johnnie Walker's Striding Man and a loyal companion as they journey around the world bringing prosperity and rejoicing in the arrival of the New Year (see Figure 6.23). The design also contains various symbols of wealth and prosperity, making this bottle extremely unique and the perfect gift to give this Chinese New Year."[41]

Figure 6.23. An example of Johnnie Walker limited edition Chinese New Year gift box. Photo credit: Amy Hsu

Everyday Occasions

Consumers generally prefer to pay less for essential items that they use on a daily basis. That's why most developed markets sell essential items in larger "economy" packs at a slightly reduced price (when the price is calculated on a per use basis) to reward consumers for buying more at one time. There is now research supporting that consumers are more likely to purchase essential items when even a modest (10 percent or lower) discount is given.[42]

Figure 6.24. Rexona sachet deodorant. Photo credit: Amy Hsu

The problem, however, is that emerging market consumers, especially in rural areas, generally have less cash on hand. This can result in higher-priced, economy-sized packaging having a negative effect on consumer demand. This is why companies like P&G and Unilever aggressively promote sachet packaging in developing rural markets as a way to lower the out-of-pocket expense of buying their brands. In India, small shampoo sachets with up to 10 ml of product make up more than 90 percent of the category's unit sales.[43]

In the Philippines, Unilever was able to penetrate the challenging rural market with Rexona deodorant by developing a cream version packaged in single-use sachets that cost about 10 cents each.

When Unilever employed the same strategy in India, Rexona cream became the brand's bestseller, doubling penetration nationwide to about 60 percent. The brand was even able to gain distribution in the smallest rural mom and pop shops as a result (see Figure 6.24 on page 139).[44]

Style Fit

A common exercise that focus group facilitators use when conducting brand research is to ask respondents to assign personality traits to the various brands under evaluation. For example, if a facilitator asked me to describe Apple, I would describe the brand as innovative, passionate, and contemporary. For Nike, I might say it is athletic, inspirational, and competitive.

As we know, just like brands, consumers have defining personality styles, and now research suggests that the brands we favor tend to reinforce our own style and self-image. Not surprisingly, research also suggests that a brand's personality can have a positive effect on purchase intention.[45]

According to David Aaker, a brand's "personality is an important dimension of brand equity because, like human personality, it is both differentiating and enduring. A brand personality can be a vehicle to express a person's self, represent relationships, and even communicate attributes."[46]

Country Personality

It stands to reason that people from different countries have different personality styles. Several studies have found that specific personality traits are expressed more in some countries. When psychologists administered personality tests to people in different countries throughout the world, they validated that the average personality in one country is often very different from the average personality in another.[47]

When Millward Brown asked more than five hundred thousand consumers to describe brands using a set of twenty-four preselected adjectives to cover a wide range of personality traits, it found that consumers from different countries viewed global brands differently using their own country's cultural lens. In Spain, the Apple iPhone is perceived as sexy and desirable, in Australia an iPhone is fun and playful, and in Japan it's creative and idealistic.[48]

This is one of the main reasons that global shoe giants Adidas and Nike have both recently adopted mega-city strategies to fuel growth. Adidas is co-creating different styles of shoes and brand communication for each of these six major metropolitan areas: New York, Los Angeles, London, Paris, Shanghai, and Tokyo. Nike is focusing on twelve key cities for its consumer direct offense: New York, London, Shanghai, Beijing, Los Angeles, Tokyo, Paris, Berlin, Mexico City, Barcelona, Seoul, and Milan.[49]

Individualism

In developing countries, when disposable income levels increase, it's common for consumers to become more individualistic. McKinsey & Company conducted surveys in China confirming that its consumers are now less willing to accept "one size fits all" solutions. Consumption choices are instead gravitating toward products and brands that better fit individual personalities.[50]

Nike is capturing share in many markets around the world with its NIKEiD platform that helps consumers customize shoes to match their individual style. In addition to its homepage, NIKEiD has 102 studios located across the globe in markets like Canada, France, England, Europe, China, and the United States where fans can access personalized design services (see Figure 6.25).

Figure 6.25. NIKEiD/Made By You, Studio, Shanghai. Photo credit: Amy Hsu

According to Ken Dice, the Global GM of NIKEiD the customization platform now generates "significant revenue and a large portion of our total e-commerce business."[51] NIKEiD permits consumers to modify more than ten different design elements with dozens of color options, names, symbols, and logos, which allows every consumer to make their pair of Nike shoes truly unique.

Group Personality Styles

In the West, we hear about Millennials being a monolithic cohort that, for example, loves technology, doesn't like hierarchy, is socially conscious and prefers direct communication. Group characteristics of Millennials can vary a lot from one country to the next. INSEAD, the HEAD Foundation, and Universum studied more than sixteen thousand millennials across forty-three countries. What they found was that Millennials from different countries, even within a specific geographic region like Asia Pacific or Wester Europe, can be as different as looking at Millennials from one region to the next.[52] The implication for global brand builders is that you can't rely on stereotypes. Instead, you need to dig deeper with more specificity when trying to uncover local consumer needs and perceptions.

Shiseido

Shiseido is a 140-year-old premium Japanese cosmetics company with the largest share of sales among Asian manufacturers. Although Shiseido has a long history and solid reputation in Japan, it has been trying for several years to change the perception that the skincare brand only caters to mature women. As CEO Masahiko Uotani stated, young "women don't have Shiseido products in their cosmetics pouches."[53]

To address this concern, Shiseido launched the "recipist" brand in Japan in 2017, and sold it primarily online, targeting Millennial women (see Figure 6.26). To create this new brand, Shiseido's New Value Creation Group conducted research to better understand what Japanese Millennial women want.

Figure 6.26. Recipist, Shiseido's skincare brand that targets Millennials. Photo credit: Amy Hsu

The team began by surveying five hundred young women about their makeup purchasing habits. Then, the team selected thirty women from the group and spent an additional twenty hours with each respondent conducting in-depth interviews, visiting their homes, and observing them using their own cosmetic products.

Kanako Kawai, who was in charge of the packaging and art direction for the project, said that the team "subdivided component elements of packaging into categories such as shape of the container, shape of the cap, color, graphic design, etc., and asked subjects to select their preferences from options offered for each element. In this way, we grasped a sense of their preferences, and incorporated these into the design."[54]

Using an ethnographic research style, the Shiseido team refined its understanding of the target and found that Japanese Millennial women:

- Place a greater importance on personal relationships.

- Cannot typically afford to spend too much on skincare, but are still very selective about their cosmetic choices.

- Value simplicity, preferring essential beauty treatments over complicated multistep programs.
- Like products made from natural ingredients.
- Place more emphasis on their senses (e.g., how product feels in their hands).
- Prioritize receiving information from people they trust.

Ryosuke Kuga, one of the primary designers participating in the research, said the "process of listening to the interviewees and analyzing their responses put this concept into words, and I felt as if I had gained a new sense of clarity and understanding."[55]

From a graphic design perspective, you can see the unique influence that "Kawaii" has on Japanese Millennial women. Kawaii is a Japanese cultural style that incorporates bright pastel colors and childlike imagery.[56] Joshua Paul Dale, a professor at Tokyo Gakugei University, writes, "Kawaii communicates the unabashed joy found in the undemanding presence of innocent, harmless, adorable things."[57]

According to Shiseido's advertising and design department, "The natural pictograms that serve as a key visual element on the packaging express the natural ingredients contained in each product, such as rose extract, raspberry extract, and pearl barley extract" (see Figure 6.27). Inspired by the success of the "recipist" development process, Shiseido recently initiated a similarly structured project, but this time it is focusing on a younger target. In January 2018, the company announced the launch of POSME, a new project and brand created with the help of Japanese high school girls.[58]

Figure 6.27. "Recipist" pictograms. Photo credit: Amy Hsu

Evian

The premium mineral water category in Japan is very competitive, and many new brands enter the market each year. To increase its appeal to Millennial women, Evian began collaborating with Japanese artists to create limited edition bottles designed specifically for Japan. In 2017, the company launched its second limited collection series with "My Little Box," a Millennial-focused brand that delivers sample boxes of cosmetics and other goods directly to Millennial women each month. The playful illustrations printed on the Evian bottles were hand drawn by Kanako, a Japanese artist/illustrator (see Figure 6.28).

To make the campaign more social, Evian introduced a meme-building site to help women create personalized "My Little Box" avatars by combining more than one hundred Kanako drawn illustrations.

Figure 6.28. The Japanese Evian "My Little Box" collaboration.
Source: Danone, used with permission

The meme site enables visitors to create images that resemble themselves by customizing eight different attributes, including eyes, mouth, skin, hair, and fashion, after which they can SMS to their friends (see Figure 6.29).

MY LITTLE BOX

Figure 6.29. An Evian Japan "My Little Box" avatar example.
Photo credit: Amy Hsu, made with *My Little Icon Maker* site

Celebrity Effect

Partnering a brand with the right celebrity can also help amplify a brand's personality. Research indicates that just announcing the use of a celebrity can increase sales by 4 percent in the immediate outcome.[59] Ipsos Connect analyzed more than 2,300 ads in a pretesting database and found that ads with a star spokesperson scored higher recall and persuasiveness than ads without a celebrity spokesperson.[60]

In Asia, the use of Korean dramas to promote brands has been an especially powerful platform for building brand associations. Because drama series unfold over a long period of time, product placements often don't come across as paid advertisements. The key is making the link natural and believable. Ideally, the product should play a role in the storyline.

Figure 6.30. Jang Dong-gun promoting Mercedes. Photo credit: Han Myung-Gu/Getty Images

Mercedes-Benz

German automotive manufacturer Mercedes-Benz has been quite success-ful using Korean dramas to enhance its brand image in Korea. The brand saw increased interest in its SUV models after being prominently featured in the drama series *A Gentlemen's Dignity*. In that series, the main character is played by actor Jang Dong-gun. He is always expressing his affection for his car that he calls "Betty," which sometimes even causes his girlfriend to get jealous (see Figure 6.30).[61] After noticing the positive effect that the drama series had on sales, Mercedes signed Jang Dong-gun to a sponsorship deal.

Korean dramas are also very popular in Mainland China, which led Mercedes Benz to reach its highest level of sales in China after the drama *My Love from the Star* featured Mercedes-Benz product placement.[62]

Coway

Coway is a leading Korean home appliance company with a mission to make consumers' lives better by designing products that improve their quality of air, water, and sleep.

The company found itself in the middle of a product recall that had the potential to shake consumer confidence in the brand. To elevate quality and trust perceptions for the brand during this critical time, Coway launched a campaign that used Korean superstar Gong Yoo.

Figure 6.31. Gong Yoo.
Photo credit: Shutterstock

Gong Yoo is a South Korean actor with a broad fan base across Asia. He became South Korea's most popular leading man after winning the Baeksang Arts Award, South Korea's equivalent of The Golden Globes (see Figure 6.31).

What makes Gong Yoo's brand especially appealing to Coway is the actor's trustworthy image within Coway's target market and direct sales force. Coway tightly linked the actor's image to a new air purifier that became the bestselling model in South Korea and Malaysia, and successfully dampened negative associations from the product recall.

Cultural Fit

Cultural fit can be tricky to assess for anyone, especially foreigners working in an unfamiliar market. This issue made an impression on me while I was working with Saatchi and Saatchi in China during a public relations crisis that resulted from an advertisement it created for Toyota (see Figure 6.32).

Saatchi produced a print ad to promote Toyota's Prado SUV in China. The ad looks benign at first glance, but Chinese consumers quickly denounced Toyota's use of Chinese stone lions (a traditional symbol of power in China) to salute the Japanese automobile in the advertisement. Chinese consumers continue to hold negative feelings toward Japan regarding incidents from World War II. To make things worse, "Prado" was translated into "Badao" in Chinese, which means "high-handed" or "domineering." The advertisement's Chinese tagline read: "You have to respect Badao."

Figure 6.32. Toyota print advertisement for Prado in China.
Photo credit: Amy Hsu

IKEA

IKEA operates in forty-seven countries and is the world's leading furniture retailer. The brand promises "to offer a wide range of well-designed, functional home furnishing products at prices so low that as many people as possible will be able to afford them."[63] IKEA's ability to deliver on this promise is differentiating and plays a large factor in the brand's global success.

One of the brand's primary forms of communication is its famous product catalogue. The IKEA catalogue is the world's largest, distributed to two hundred million homes and read by more than five hundred million potential consumers.[64] Each year, the brand creates seventy-two regional versions in thirty-two different languages. Although much of the content remains the same for each region, IKEA adapts details to cater to cultural differences.

Figure 6.33. IKEA catalogue comparison of kitchens in the United States (left) compared to China (right). Photo credit: Amy Hsu

A variety of ninja research techniques are used so the brand can gain insights to adapt to cultural needs. Prior to producing a catalogue, IKEA conducts ethnographies in every major market by visiting thousands of homes in each region to observe consumers and experience how they live. The team takes what they learned and uses the information to make adaptations to the global catalogue. Mikael Ydholm, head of research for IKEA, says, "The more far away we go from our culture, the more we need to understand, learn, and adapt."[65]

Greater China is an extremely important market for the brand because eight of the world's ten largest volume IKEA stores are located there. So it's important that Chinese consumers can relate to what is pictured in the catalogue. In 2017, the Chinese catalogue team digitally modified pictures of home kitchens to more closely reflect the smaller ones typically found in Chinese homes (see Figure 6.33 on page 151).[66]

In another example of adapting to meet local cultural needs, IKEA sent members of Israel's Haredi community a catalogue with a front cover that featured challah boards, Shabbat candlesticks, Sabbath table settings, and bookcases lined with the Talmud book of Jewish civil and ceremonial law (see Figure 6.34).[67]

Figure 6.34. Israeli's Haredi community catalogue cover.
Photo credit: Amy Hsu

What's in a Name?

When launching a global brand into a local market, make sure your brand name doesn't translate with negative connotations. This task should be at the top of your to-do list. This is best illustrated by Geoffrey James, a contributing editor for Inc.com, who created a list of the twenty worst examples of brands neglecting to take this crucial first step:

1. Braniff International's translation of a slogan touting its finely upholstered seats "Fly in Leather" read as "Fly Naked" in Spanish.

2. Clairol launched a curling iron called "Mist Stick" in Germany where the word "mist" is slang for manure.

3. Coca-Cola's brand name, when first marketed in China, was sometimes translated as "Bite the Wax Tadpole."

4. Colgate launched toothpaste named "Cue" in France without realizing that it's also the name of a pornographic magazine.

5. Coors translated its slogan, "Turn It Loose," into Spanish, where it is a colloquial term for having diarrhea.

6. Electrolux once marketed vacuum cleaners in the United States with the tagline "Nothing sucks like an Electrolux."

7. Ford blundered when marketing its Pinto to the Brazilian auto market because the term in Portuguese means "tiny male genitals."

8. Frank Perdue's tagline, "It takes a tough man to make a tender chicken," translated into Spanish as "It takes a sexually stimulated man to make a chicken affectionate."

9. Gerber marketed baby food in Africa with a baby pictured on the label without understanding that products there have pictures of the ingredients because many consumers can't read.

10. IKEA products were marketed in Thailand with Swedish names that in the Thai language mean "sex" and "getting to third base."

11. KFC made Chinese consumers a bit apprehensive when "finger lickin' good" was translated as "eat your fingers off."

12. Mercedes-Benz entered the Chinese market under the brand name "Bensi," which means "rush to die."

13. Nike had to recall thousands of products when illustrations on the back of the shoes intended to picture fire resembled the Arabic word for Allah.

14. In Japan, Panasonic launched a Web-ready PC with a Woody Woodpecker theme using the slogan "Touch Woody: The Internet Pecker."

15. Parker Pen, when expanding into Mexico, mistranslated "It won't leak in your pocket and embarrass you" into "It won't leak in your pocket and make you pregnant."

16. Paxam, an Iranian consumer goods company, brands its laundry soap with "Barf," which means "snow" in Farsi, resulting in packages labeled "Barf Soap."

17. Pepsi's slogan "Pepsi Brings You Back to Life" was debuted in China as "Pepsi Brings You Back from the Grave."

18. Puffs marketed its tissues under that brand name in Germany even though "puff" is slang for a brothel.

19. The American Dairy Association replicated its "Got Milk?" campaign in Spanish-speaking countries where it was translated as "Are You Lactating?"

20. Vicks introduced its cough drops into the German market without realizing that the German pronunciation of "v" is "f," making "Vicks" slang for sexual intercourse.[68]

Calpis or Calpico?

This is one of my favorite brand name adaptation stories. The Calpis brand is owned by Asahi Soft Drinks and is the leading lactobacillus beverage brand sold in Japan. Exported to more than 110 countries, the brand is especially popular with children because of its sweet yogurty flavor. According to Calpis, the name (pronounced cow-piss) is derived from "Cal," which stands for calcium, and "pis," which stands for salpis, a Sanskrit word that refers to milk fermentation.

In 1991, Calpis began distributing product in the United Sates. As expected, American consumers found the original Japanese name a bit unappetizing, so it was changed to Calpico to avoid confusion and negative brand associations (see Figure 6.35).

Figure 6.35. Calpico and Calpis soda. Photo credit: Amy Hsu

Oreo Cookies in China

When entering a developing market, you first need to assess how consumers will evaluate your brand when they view it through their cultural lens. Never assume your new consumers will react the same way your consumers did back home. Not only will there be cultural differences, but the consumer care-abouts will have evolved from what was important back when the brand got its start.

Oreo cookies were first sold in the United States back in 1912. From the very beginning, Oreos were made by sandwiching rich vanilla frosting between two small round chocolate cookies. It did not take long for Oreo to become the bestselling cookie in America. For decades, even before it was the official brand slogan, Oreo cookies were known as "America's best loved cookie."

Searching for more growth, Oreo launched into China in 1996, and believed it could just reapply what had worked so well in the United States. Unfortunately, it would not be that simple. Oreo struggled to gain momentum and even contemplated pulling out at one point. Luckily, before it failed, the team fielded consumer research to better understand local food culture and the cookie category in China.

Figure 6.36. Examples of Oreo cookies from China.
Photo credit: Tang Yan Song/Shutterstock

Oreo learned that Chinese consumers were generally not that excited about the taste of the original Oreo cookie. Many thought that the filling was too sweet and that the chocolate cookie was too bitter.[69] More importantly, the Oreo team learned that Chinese consumers were at a different stage in the category's lifecycle.

Chinese consumers wanted Oreos to deliver an experience in exchange for a premium price. The classic Oreo cookie just wasn't unique enough. So, Oreo reformulated its classic cookie recipe and reintroduced it with a range of new flavors that wowed consumers. Oreo's new offerings included green tea ice cream, raspberry/blueberry, mango/orange, and grape/peach. Oreo also extended the brand into the popular wafer format, which is extremely popular (see Figure 6.36 on page 156). To differentiate Oreo's offering and appeal to local needs, the brand raised the bar. Chinese Oreos combine multiple tastes and textures to provide an entertaining eating experience.

Kit Kat Japan

Sometimes a brand's global positioning only needs a slight adjustment to take advantage of local cultural perceptions. That was the case for Kit Kat in Japan.

Kit Kat is a British-born chocolate wafer brand owned by Nestlé. The brand got its start in England in 1937, and slowly expanded distribution to other Western markets like Australia, New Zealand, South Africa, and Canada throughout the 1940s. It was during this time period that the global brand messaging coalesced around the pleasure of taking a break with Kit Kat. Kit Kat bars contain three layers of wafer that are covered with an inner and outer layer of chocolate. The original Kit Kat bar had four fingers that could be broken apart before eating.

Kit Kat arrived in Japan in 1973 with modest sales, but everything changed in 1990 when Kit Kat launched strawberry-flavored Kit Kat in Hokkaido, Japan. Hokkaido is a popular tourist destination for the Japanese, and the team was inspired to add variety to the kinds of snacks sold in Hokkaido souvenir shops. The experiment paid off as the team discovered that Kit Kat bars were perfect for gifting, because the bars are wrapped in bright, colorful single-serve packs just like traditional Japanese snacks. When the Kit Kat team began adding more Japanese-specific flavors like matcha green tea, Shinshu apple, and Hokkaido melon, sales started to take off. Kit Kat sales in Japan grew 50 percent between 2010 and 2016.[70]

Another adaptation that the Kit Kat Japan team made was playing on how the brand name in Japanese sounds similar to "kitto katsu," which roughly translates into "to certainly win."[71] The Japanese brand team made the link even stronger by encouraging consumers to give Kit Kat bars to students before exams for good luck.

Nestlé's Global Head of Confectionery, Sandra Martinez, said in an interview that "Japan is the market that has made Kit Kat so iconic in terms of all the different flavors they've developed."[72] Kit Kat is now the number-one chocolate brand in Japan's $5 billion chocolate confectionery market and one of Kit Kat's largest markets globally. To date, Nestlé has launched more than three hundred different varieties of Kit Kat bars into Japan (see Figure 6.37).

Figure 6.37. Examples of Kit Kat bars from Japan.
Photo credit: gnoparus/Shutterstock

Relative Price

Even though consumers in developing countries generally have less income than shoppers in developed markets, the price of purchasing global products in developing markets usually remains expensive because of the high costs associated with building global brands.

Too often, there is little flexibility for the global brand to adapt pricing. The question inevitably becomes: How can you build new brand associations to help increase the perceived value of your brand, so price becomes less of a barrier to trial? Because value is a function of perceived benefits and price (e.g., Value = Benefits – Price), if you cannot lower the price, you have to increase the perceived benefits.

Starbucks

In 1999, Starbucks opened its first Mainland China location in Beijing. As discussed in Chapter 2, Starbucks positioned itself as an experience in China. This was a smart move from a strategic perspective because it is much harder for a consumer to gauge the value of an experience versus a cup of coffee, and the experience adds perceived benefits to the cup of coffee.[73]

What follows is a translated radio advertisement that aired in the early days of Starbucks' launch into China. In some ways, by positioning the brand as an experience, the price of a cup of coffee becomes an entry fee to gain access to the store experience.

> You can see crowded passengers out of the window, and inside, you are sharing peace and comfort with your dear coffee. We know what you want. It is the life, and love to the life. Enjoy the life, your public space, Starbucks.[74]

Up until today, the brand continues to build on the concept of delivering an experience as evidenced by the values statement taken from the Starbucks China website:

> With our partners, coffee and customers at the core, we strive to practice the following values: Create a culture of warmth and belonging where everyone is welcome.[75]

Another way that Starbucks is changing its perceived value in China is by encouraging consumers to join the My Starbucks Rewards program

Figure 6.38. WeChat Starbucks campaign in China. Photo credit: Amy Hsu

via the WeChat payment platform, which allows those who sign up to earn "stars" that can later be redeemed for products. The WeChat payment platform seamlessly integrates with the My Starbucks Rewards program that launched in China in 2016 and already has more than twelve million users.[76]

According to Belinda Wong, CEO of Starbucks China, "WeChat Pay has already reached a remarkable 29 percent of tender and has elevated the Starbucks Experience for both customers and partners through its convenience and fast transaction speed. We saw growth in all categories and dayparts" (see Figure 6.38 on page 160).[77]

Tesla

In 2016, Tesla's China sales tripled from the previous year, which helped the company earn $1.1 billion in revenue from the China market alone.[78] Tesla is managing to grow sales despite being more expensive than local electric vehicles and higher than Tesla cars sold in the United States. Because Tesla cars are manufactured in the United States, they are subject to additional costs that do not apply to locally made vehicles, such as a 10 percent sales tax, 25 percent tariff, and the extra cost of shipping a Tesla all the way from California to China.[79]

In response, Tesla is encouraging Chinese consumers to consider the total cost of buying and owning one of its electric vehicles. By doing this, the brand can reframe the price conversation.

Local Chinese dealerships typically inflate the list price of imported cars like BMW, Audi, and Mercedes-Benz by tens of thousands of dollars, adding various fees on top of the advertised price. Tesla's innovative direct sales showrooms do not add fees, thereby reducing the stress involved in making a new car purchase. The company also emphasizes the savings a consumer can expect to enjoy as an owner of a Tesla compared to a gasoline-fueled car during the life of the vehicle, including the benefits of having access to Tesla's easy maintenance and charging services.

Nevertheless, what's proving to be one of the most impactful factors in increasing perceived value is the differentiated image of Tesla. Like Apple stores, Tesla showrooms are modern and fun to visit compared to traditional luxury car showrooms (see Figure 6.39). Tesla has even built eighteen "experience centers" in China where schoolchildren can come on field trips to learn about science, electric vehicles, and green energy.[80] The brand has been rigorously promoting its "green" positioning in China. As a result, the Tesla brand is now associated with being young, technologically savvy, and on-trend in China.

By occupying a foreign/aspirational space in the minds of consumers, Tesla has made its price point less relevant. In many ways, Tesla now finds itself competing against luxury gas-powered vehicles in China, instead of locally madeelectric-powered cars.[81]

Figure 6.39. Tesla showroom in a Chinese luxury shopping mall.
Photo credit: Amy Hsu

Plan Your Attack

1. Identify the attributes that influence purchase intent for product category and determine which attributes to adapt or standardize.

2. Use the brand adaptation framework to determine which attributes should be amplified and which should be dampened.

3. Look for associations that you can build that would negatively affect how consumers perceive a competitive brand or positively perceive your brand.

Part 3
Bring It to Life

Step Up and Disrupt

7

"*Obstacles don't have to stop you. If you run into a wall, don't turn around and give up. Figure out how to climb it, go through it, or work around it.*"
–Michael Jordan

"*There is no spoon.*"
–Neo from *The Matrix*

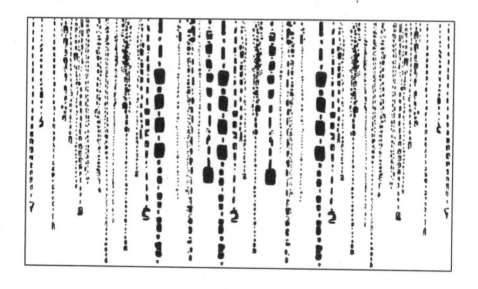

recently moved to the Bay Area to be at the epicenter of all the disruptive innovation being generated in Silicon Valley. "Disruption" has unfortunately become somewhat of a dirty word for many these days, conjuring up images of ruthless tech companies making traditional business models obsolete. Being a lean marketer, my view of disruption gravitates toward a classic definition. Revisiting my ninja metaphor, ninja fighters were skilled disruptors of conventional warfare, allowing them to successfully combat larger, established armies. According to Clayton Christensen, a professor from Harvard Business School, "disruption" in a business context describes a process whereby a smaller company with fewer resources is able to successfully challenge an established incumbent business.[1]

Disruptive Growth, Startup Growth

Leveraging disruptive technology is not a new idea. In fact, one of the key factors that contributed to the early success of McDonald's in the United States was its decision to place stores where it could take advantage of the emerging interstate highway system. President Eisenhower's Federal Aid Highway Act of 1956 created 41,000 miles of new interstate highway and lots of hungry drivers looking for a clean and convenient place to stop and take a break.[2] McDonald's leveraged the expanding interstate highway platform and strategically placed its restaurants next to interstate off-ramps. The rest, as we all now know, is fast-food history.

In Chapter 5, we looked at the history of the Minute Maid brand. One of the key reasons the brand became so successful in the United States was because it was the first juice company to leverage a new type of freezing technology. This innovation allowed the brand to distribute "fresh" tasting orange juice throughout the entire country, regardless of the season.

The Minute Maid launch in China once again took advantage of new technology. This time, Coca-Cola developed a manufacturing process that enabled the juice to create a "pulpy" texture that emulates the consistency of fresh orange juice while reducing expensive juice content to 10 percent.

Equidam, a leading provider of online business valuation services, surveyed more than fifteen thousand companies in seventy-eight countries ranging from high-tech startups to well-established businesses. Equidam found that the average company forecasts an amazing 120 percent growth after year one, 82 percent after year two, and 60 percent after year three.[3] Now contrast that to the historically low average sales growth rate for the S&P 500, which is roughly 3 percent annually.[4]

It makes perfect sense that businesses just getting off the ground can achieve higher growth rates because they are starting from a much smaller base. However, as companies become more established, it becomes harder for them to continue to grow at that same rate.

Adopt Disruptive Technology

In 2018, Tesla forecasted 33 percent annual growth,[5] while Airbnb predicted it would double its annual stays,[6] and Uber's bookings have been growing at more than 100 percent a year.[7] Each of these companies entered a well-established category like automobile manufacturing, transportation, and hospitality, and then disrupted the status quo.

In much the same way, when you are building a new brand in a developing or emerging market, you have the rare opportunity to quickly adopt disruptive technology and create a step change in the traditional growth curve.

Existing brands often get stuck focusing on maximizing the return on the investments they have already made, motivated by incentives to do business in the same way they always have.

According to a 2018 survey of top US marketers by Deloitte, Duke, the Florida School of Business, and the American Marketing Association, marketing budgets only increased 7.3 percent in the past twelve months. They were expected to improve marginally to 10.9 percent in the following year.[8]

However, it takes a lot more than increasing 10 percent here or optimizing 10 percent there to create a step change in growth. The good news is, as a new market entrant, you are less likely to be anchored to legacy investments. That means you have more freedom to ride disruptive technologies that can give you a competitive advantage.

Today there are many disruptive platforms that can become a catalyst for step-change growth, but if you want to create a competitive advantage, you must act early and fast. The problem is not predicting which technology will affect your brand but selecting which technology's growth you can ride on. That's why it is important to stay current on emerging technologies, especially those outside of your product category.

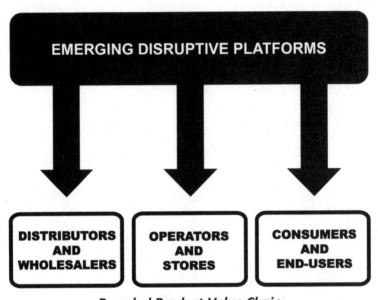

-Branded Product Value Chain-

Figure 7.1. Applying disruptive platforms to the branded product value chain.

Although it may seem that some of these platforms have been around for a long time, continuous improvements in functionality and reductions in technology costs have pushed many of them to the tipping point. Examine the links in your brand's value chain and ideate with your team on how you can add value to each link by leveraging a potentially disruptive platform (see Figure 7.1).

In the following section, I have listed many platforms that have the potential to be disruptive when entering an emerging or developing market. Nevertheless, you should begin compiling your own list that you can add to whenever you come across a new technology that you believe has potential.

Internet of Everything

The Internet of Everything (IoE) refers to how more and more products are designed to allow them to be intelligently connected to each other and the Internet. Imagine a future where everything is connected, facilitating communication and learning between people, people and things, and even between things themselves.

The analyst firm Gartner says that in the near future there will be more than twenty billion connected devices.[9] Intel's estimate is even higher, forecasting two hundred billion connected devices for the same time frame. That would equate to about twenty-six smart devices for every man, woman, and child on the planet.[10]

There is no doubt that the implications for IoE will be far-reaching and provide a catalyst for creating disruptive value for brands entering new markets. The following are a few examples showing how brands leverage IoE.

Coca-Cola Freestyle

One of the primary challenges that global brands face in developing markets is obtaining visibility on who their end-users are—gaining a clear picture of consumers so brand builders can use that understanding to provide meaningful, brand-building content and solutions.

Coca-Cola's Freestyle platform received a lot of attention for offering more than one hundred different flavor options to consumers, as well as allowing consumers to create their own recipes. What often gets overlooked in all the excitement is Freestyle's ability to communicate data back to Coca-Cola and other stakeholders such as restaurants and retailers.

The Freestyle machine uses microdosing technology and flavor cartridges that resemble the ink cartridges found in color laser printers. Because Freestyle machines are connected to the Internet, they are able to automatically place orders for replacement cartridges and other supplies to reduce the losses that result from out-of-stocks. Additionally, the machine is designed to introduce new beverage flavors with a simple overnight software update. Consumers can even download a mobile app that allows them to save and share their favorite creations using Quick Response (QR) codes (see Figure 7.2).

Figure 7.2. The Coca-Cola Freestyle App with more than one hundred choices. Photo credit: Amy Hsu

Armed with consumer usage data, Coca-Cola can introduce new flavors that have been "co-created" and validated by real consumers.[11] Recently, Coca-Cola North America launched Sprite Cherry and Sprite Cherry Zero into retail shops based on data obtained from the Freestyle platform. Bobby Oliver, director of Sprite and citrus brands in North America, said, "The fact that cherry was the number-one Sprite flavor mix on Coca-Cola Freestyle inspired us to create an all-new, delicious product for fans in a convenient, on-the-go bottle."[12]

East-West Seed

East-West Seed (EWS) is a leading global seed manufacturer headquartered in Thailand, specializing in serving the needs of small vegetable farmers around the world. The company's mission is to help farmers improve the quality of their lives and the communities they live in. So it is not an exaggeration to say that EWS is doing something very important for the world. It's estimated that roughly 2.4 billion small farmers produce about 70 percent of all the food that is eaten worldwide. It's also forecasted that by 2050, the world will need to feed an additional 2 billion people.[13]

Putting aside the daunting implications associated with the population surge, if we only consider the effects of rising income, rural migration, and global climate change, it becomes very clear that small farmers will need all the help that they can get.

EWS relies on a distribution network to resell its seeds to sub distributors who then pass the seeds on to an estimated eighteen million farmers worldwide, but how does EWS support eighteen million farmers when they only have about four thousand employees?[14] Like many global brands operating in developing and emerging markets, EWS finds it difficult to gain visibility on such a large number of end-users (small farmers). So, the brand needed to find a way to communicate directly to small farmers in order to provide meaningful content and listen to their needs.

With mobile phone and data prices continuing to fall in developing markets, roughly 37 percent of the population now owns smartphones in nondeveloped markets.[15] The number is even higher in Southeast Asia, with mobile Internet users making up nearly 50 percent of the total population.[16] As a result, the prevalence of using phones for online activities once reserved for laptops and desktops is rising. In Africa, researchers are now predicting that mobile Internet usage will increase twenty-fold over the next five years. That's double the rate of growth we are seeing in the rest of the world.[17]

Seeing an opportunity to leverage the growth in smartphone usage, EWS created a "Knowledge Transfer" and "CropWiki" app for small farmers. Using these apps, the farmer can upload crop information, photos, and notes. Then, based on that information, EWS helps to provide digital training to farmers on good agronomic practices to help increase yields (see Figure 7.3).[18]

According to a Rithea Heng of EWS, the brand must engage "in knowledge transfer because having good quality seeds is not enough to make vegetable farming profitable. Good agronomic practices are essential to maximize the genetic potential of the varieties we introduce."

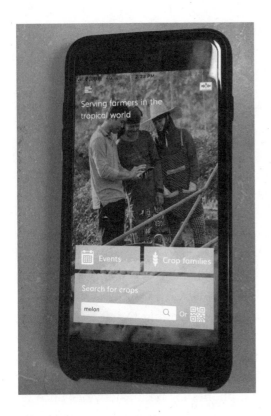

Figure 7.3. East-West Seed Crop Wiki mobile app. Photo credit: Amy Hsu

McCain Foods India

McCain Foods, headquartered in Canada, is primarily a B2B food brand, operating in 160 countries worldwide. Like East-West Seed, McCain is using IoE technology to help improve the lives of small farmers in India.

McCain supplies French fries to McDonald's in India. According to McCain, it manufactures one out of every three French fries eaten around the world, with annual global sales exceeding $6 billion USD.[19]

India has the world's largest youth population with 356 million people between the ages of ten and twenty-four, making it a very important market for McDonald's.[20] Prior to McCain entering India, McDonald's was forced to use expensive foreign-produced fries to meet its strict global quality standards. In an effort to improve the quality of locally manufactured French fries, McCain began working with Indian farmers on potato crop quality through better seed selection, sowing, irrigation, and harvesting techniques (see Figure 7.4).

Figure 7.4. Typical small farmer potato cultivation in India.
Photo credit: Tuktuki | Dreamstime

These changes helped farmers not only increase their yield, but also resulted in a higher quality potato that required less water for irrigation. Because McCain purchases their potatoes directly from small farmers, it was able to eliminate the middlemen or "mandi," resulting in more demand certainty and better margins for the farmers.[21]

In India, McDonald's is positioned as a value offering, and routinely asks suppliers like McCain to reduce ingredient costs to help it remain competitive. Meeting McDonald's cost-reduction demands required McCain to achieve a step-change in efficiency. There are many factors that need to be monitored by small farmers that ultimately affect crop yield, such as the type of seeds used, planting techniques, air temperature, humidity, irrigation, fertilizers, and pesticides. [22]

The typical small farmer in India records farming data manually, which can lead to inconsistent record keeping and lower crop yields due to bad decisions made from using bad data. McCain partnered with Cropin, an Indian digital farm management provider, to geo-tag plots and install digital sensors that can detect dew point, rainfall, frost, and other challenges associated with farming potatoes.

By leveraging IoE technology, McCain gained more visibility of field activities and the ability to monitor crop conditions through an interactive dashboard. All of this results in better decision-making and an increase in potato farming yields.[23]

7-Eleven Japan

Radio Frequency Identification (RFID) systems have long been used by companies like Zara to help manage global inventories and increase supply chain efficiencies. RFID technology uses radio waves to identify tagged objects. RFID tags contain an integrated circuit and built-in antenna that can transmit data to a reader at distances of up to 30 feet without physical contact or line of sight (see Figure 7.5).[24]

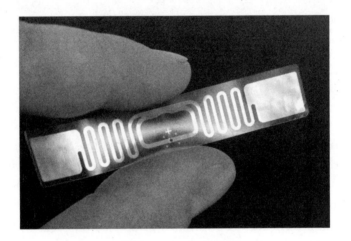

Figure 7.5. An example of an RFID tag.
Photo credit: Audrius Merfeldas, Shutterstock

7-Eleven is the largest convenience store chain in the world with a network of more than sixty-four thousand stores. In Japan, a country with an estimated fifty-five thousand convenience stores, there are nearly twenty thousand 7-Eleven stores in operation.[25]

Each 7-Eleven store requires roughly twenty part-time workers.[26] Unfortunately, c-store chains in Japan are finding it increasingly difficult to hire enough employees because of a dwindling labor force stemming from an aging and shrinking population.

C-store workers need to be good at multitasking. In addition to ringing up merchandise, they also keep track of what's in inventory, place products on shelves, and help keep the stores clean. The large amount of work combined with a shortage of employees inevitably leads to situations in which service quality becomes sacrificed. To help remedy this, 7-Eleven Japan aims to automate all convenience stores by 2025 with a new RFID technology.[27]

Integrating RFID technology will allow 7-Eleven consumers to check out an entire basket of items at one time instead of scanning each item separately.[28] The hope is that this new process will not only decrease the amount of labor required, but also speed up customer transactions (see Figures 7.6 and 7.7).

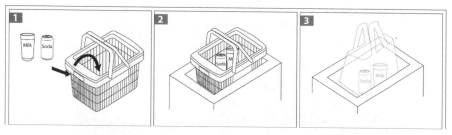

Figure 7.6. How the newest RFID self-checkout machines work.
Photo credit: John 062

Figure 7.7. An example of a new RFID automated checkout system that is being tested in Japan. Source: Panasonic, used with permission

Homeplus

When Tesco, a leading global retailer with more than six thousand shops around the world entered South Korea, the company created a new brand for the local market named Homeplus. The new brand eventually grew to become the country's second largest retailer behind E-Mart.[29]

With fewer stores than E-Mart, Homeplus needed to find a way to step-change its penetration and close the gap. The company believed the answer might be in the high usage of smartphones within the South Korean population. According to the Pew Research Center, 88 percent of adults living in South Korea own a smartphone. That's the highest smartphone ownership rate anywhere in the world.[30]

Homeplus responded by creating a "virtual" store campaign in subway stations using printed billboards that displayed ranges of products and corresponding QR codes. These printed displays were made to look just like product shelves found in "real" Homeplus stores (see Figure 7.8). Consumers scan a QR code with their mobile phone and the product gets automatically added to their shopping cart and delivered right to their front door later in the day.

Figure 7.8. South Koreans "virtually shopping" in a subway station.
Photo credit: Jackmalipan | Dreamstime

Homeplus was able to break through the competitive clutter and encourage consumers to stop and re-evaluate the brand. The brand demonstrated to South Korean consumers how online shopping could be more convenient than visiting a real store. As a result, the virtual stores received more than nine hundred thousand app downloads in less than a year, driving substantial online sales growth. Because of these virtual stores, the number of new registered Homeplus app members rose by 76 percent and online sales increased 130 percent. Homeplus has now become South Korea's number-one online retailer.[31]

Ofo

Ofo is the brand behind those canary-yellow bicycles you find on streets all over China (see Figure 7.9). Launched in 2015, Ofo at one point operated more than ten million share-bikes in China and another one hundred thousand bikes in more than nineteen countries around the world.[32]

Share-bike systems are not a new idea. Over a decade ago in Europe, brands like Vélo'v, Vélib, and Bicing were pioneers in creating large-scale share-bike systems. However, brands like Ofo, Mobike, and Hellobike in China created a step-change in usage by leveraging IoE technology to create dockless bike-sharing systems. The problem with the original bike-sharing systems was that they were inconvenient. Bikes had to be retrieved and returned to specific docking stations, often requiring users to walk long distances to reach their final destinations.

With the new systems, riders just need to download an app that helps them locate a bike nearby and then use the app to unlock the bike and begin their journey. When they arrive at their final destination, they can park the bike in any spot that is legal and lock it using an app.

Because the underlying technology has become more accessible, brands in this space need to remain agile. Competing for market share, some brands are finding success by combining several services under one app. For example, Didi, China's equivalent of Uber, recently purchased Bluegogo, a bike-sharing platform, to provide additional convenience and increase barriers to entry. According to Tu Le, founder of consulting firm Sino Auto Insights, people want to use one app to hail everything: scooters, bikes, and cars: "That's where the sweet spot's going to be."[33]

Figure 7.9. Ofo bikes parked in front of a subway entrance in Fuzhou, China.
Photo credit: StreetVJ/Shutterstock

Effective Customer Relationship Management (CRM)

Customer Relationship Management (CRM) is a term used in business to describe IT platforms that store customer data and interactions, so companies can more effectively manage customer relationships.

Although CRM platforms have been around since the 1990s, their ability to disrupt has recently reached an inflection point with the integration of mobile devices, e-commerce, social communities, and email marketing. The following 4S framework was developed to help illustrate to my teams the potential of integrated CRM platforms (see Figure 7.10).

In emerging markets, distribution can be highly fragmented at the wholesale and street level. Sales teams must often manage extremely large geographic areas and portfolios of accounts, which results in limited mental bandwidth to support large numbers of customers. With an integrated CRM system, sales teams can gain important visibility of purchases and activities even at the street level. A good system enables salespeople to respond promptly to requests made by customers. However, what is really exciting about today's CRM platforms is the ability to integrate emerging digital technologies to drive demand. Now, let's examine each leg of the 4S framework.

4S CRM FRAMEWORK

SEE	SPEAK	SELL	SERVICE
IDENTIFY AND CONNECT WITH END-USERS	DELIVER TARGETED CONTENT AND PRODUCT INFO	RECOMMEND PRODUCTS AND BUNDLES	VIRTUAL TRAINING AND DEMONSTRATIONS
LEARN ABOUT NEEDS AND INSIGHTS	EDUCATE AND BUILD BRAND ASSOCIATIONS	PLACE ORDERS AND ACCEPT PAYMENT	LOYALTY PROGRAMS AND SALES MATERIALS

Figure 7.10. 4S CRM/E-commerce framework.

The 4S Framework Examined

SEE the End-User

◆ Take advantage of every opportunity to collect information from end-users (consumers) on packaging, during product demonstrations, presentations, trade shows, and sampling events.

◆ Make data more actionable by analyzing and segmenting the information that is gathered based on demographics and purchase behavior.

SPEAK to the End-User

◆ Create targeted content to build positive brand associations and engage directly with different segments of consumers using tailored messages.

- Time the delivery of brand messages to coincide with when users will be the most receptive—for example, based on seasons, consumer trends, and the Buyer Decision Cycle (see Figure 7.11).

- Send information about new product launches and limited-time-offers (LTO) directly to end-users with incentives to buy.

- Invite target users to participate in brand promotions and contribute to online communities.

- Deliver KOL communication.

SELL to End-Users

- Based on end-user data and purchase history, suggest products and remind users about items that need replenishing.

- Collect orders, payments, and delivery instructions.

- Deliver post-purchase reinforcement messages.

SERVICE End-Users

- Offer rewards and value-added services to increase perceived value and encourage repeat business and loyalty.

- Provide online training modules and virtual demonstrations.

- Customize point of sales (POS) and training materials.

- Solicit feedback and offer expert consultation.

Buyer Decision Cycle

The Buyer Decision Cycle describes the journey a buyer takes before and after purchasing a brand.

Buyers need to be aware of a brand choice before the brand can become part of a buyer's consideration set. When the brand is under consideration, the buyer can evaluate the brand value proposition against the competitive set before making a final decision to purchase.

After making a purchase, the buyer enters a relationship with the brand, deciding whether or not to repeat. As the relationship grows, the bond becomes stronger or weaker, leading to deeper emotions such as loyalty or love.

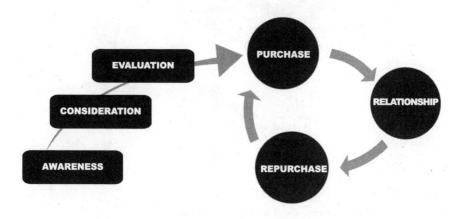

Figure 7.11. The Buyer Decision Cycle.

Coca-Cola Germany

Coca-Cola Germany created an integrated CRM system that is disrupting the beverage industry in Germany by providing fully connected CRM applications to its distributors, retailers, and customers. The system increases the effectiveness of Coca-Cola's stakeholders by giving them access to data, devices, and customer interactions in real time.

Coca-Cola created an integrated mobile app that helps sales reps plan, prepare, and execute meetings with customers more quickly and with more accuracy (see Figure 7.12).

The mobile app also has a virtual reality (VR) function that leverages customer data to show retailers exactly how Coca-Cola products will look merchandised in their stores.

Figure 7.12. Strategy Deployment Smart CRM—360°.
Source: Genetsis Partners, used with permission

Coca-Cola Germany has experienced the following results from using integrated CRM technology:

- +27 percent increase in sales revenues
- +34 percent increase in sales productivity
- +42 percent increase in forecast accuracy[34]

When asked about its CRM platform, Coca-Cola Germany's CEO Ulrik Nehammer said, "It's a very important time in history to have a great brand coupled with great technology. We are on to something very, very special. Some would call it a secret formula."[35]

Domino's Australia

Domino's Pizza Enterprises, the largest pizza chain in Australia, decided to leverage emerging digital technology to step-change the brand's growth trajectory. It started by focusing on online ordering, which makes up more than half of the company's sales.

Domino's looked to leverage the growth in smartphone usage to appeal to a younger generation of consumers who are connected to their smartphones and social media—and who demanded exceptionally fast service, online and off.[36] Don Meij, the CEO of Domino's Pizza Enterprises said, "From a Domino's perspective, the great thing about mobile is that it puts a pizza store in everybody's pocket. So you can order a Domino's pizza anywhere, anytime, anyplace on any kind of mobile smartphone device."[37]

Domino's began by developing mobile applications for smartphones and tablets. In 2014, the company added a voice-ordering assistant to the mobile ordering app that guides consumers through the ordering process using natural-language technology.[38] In 2015, Domino's followed up by adding GPS tracking so consumers could track their driver from the store to their door, launched a two-tap ordering option for smart watches, and launched text messaging and Twitter ordering platforms (see Figure 7.13).[39]

Figure 7.13. Domino's large portfolio of digital ordering platforms.
Source: DPE, used with permission

Domino's claims that its focus on disruptive technology in Australia and New Zealand helped drive 17 percent growth in both revenue and same store sales.[40]

Augmented Reality (AR)

Thanks to continuous advancements in mobile computing power, augmented reality (AR) is finally reaching an inflection point. Apple's new AR technology, ARKit, is a perfect example of the progress being made.

Apple has embedded sensors and software into its new iPhones and operating system that allows developers to create apps that utilize those AR capabilities. The ARKit hardware and software can map and make sense of what the iPhone detects around the user in the real world and then lays virtual objects on top of it.[41]

Unlike virtual reality (VR), AR only requires a newer AR ready smartphone making it very easy for consumers to adopt the technology. Tim Cook, Apple's CEO, made a bold prediction regarding VR's role in business when doing an interview with *Vogue* magazine: "Last month, IKEA and Anthropologie released new versions on their apps that allow customers to see how a new chair or lamp might look in their living rooms—and in the latter's case, even sample different fabrics and colors. Over time, I think [these features] will be as key as having a website."[42]

To piggyback on what Cook said, it is clear that AR will become extremely meaningful to consumers living in developing and emerging markets where product distribution is often fragmented and lacking depth. In these situations, AR can enable consumers to virtually try things before buying them, effectively lowering many barriers to trial. Consumers will benefit from this technology when evaluating a wide range of products and services, such as trying on new clothing or a pair of eyeglasses, experimenting with different kinds of makeup, or buying new furniture for their homes.

Converse

Converse was one of the first brands to use AR technology to make it easier to buy shoes online. The Sampler iPhone app by Converse was very simple to use. To imagine what you would look like wearing a new pair of Converse, you select a pair of shoes on the app and then point your phone at your leg. Instantaneously, you could see what it would look like to wear the shoe you selected (see Figure 7.14).[43]

Figure 7.14. The Sampler iPhone app by Converse.
Source: WeAR Studio, used with permission

Topology Eyewear

Topology Eyewear uses advanced AR technology that takes a 3-D scan of a face with an iPhone app and then lets the potential buyer virtually try on different frames without stepping into a store. Each eyeglass frame from Topology is bespoke, matching the precise measurements of a user's face (see Figure 7.15).

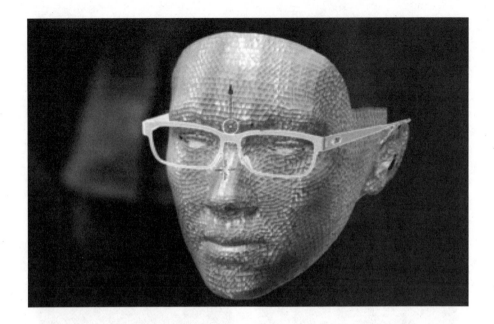

Figure 7.15. Three-dimensional facial scanning to custom fit eyewear.
Source: Topology Eyewear, used with permission

Consumers are able to customize the color, lenses, and materials to meet specific tastes and needs. Before an order is finalized, users can share their creation via text or social media with friends to solicit feedback, reducing the anxiety associated with buying a new pair of glasses and saving a lot of time.[44]

Sephora

Sephora is owned by the French luxury conglomerate LVMH and has more than 2,300 stores in thirty-three countries around the world.[45] Sephora uses AR to keep consumers in its stores longer. Sephora knows that the longer consumers stay in the store, the more money they will spend. So, the brand step-changed the shopping experience compared to what is typically offered at department store beauty counters.

Sephora strives to create a playground for Millennial women by allowing visitors to stay as long as they want—there is no hard sell. The brand uses AR and RFID technology to empower guests to pick up items and "tap and try" using Sephora's Visual Artist software located throughout the store. In addition, guests have access to Sephora's Skincare IQ diagnostic software that determines the best products for their skin.[46]

International consumers especially love the technology and "play" format because less information gets lost in translation and the consumer owns the experience. Calvin McDonald, president and CEO of Sephora Americas, said, "When a client comes in and experiences Teach, Inspire, Play, she's going to experience it on her own, she's going to experience it through cast members, and she's going to experience it through technology" (see Figures 7.16. and 7.17).[47]

Figure 7.16. Photo of Sephora Virtual Artist interface. Photo credit: Amy Hsu

Figure 7.17. "Sephora Bar" play area in Shanghai, China.
Photo credit: Amy Hsu

IKEA

Taking a trip to IKEA to buy furniture can require a big time investment. Not only does it take time to travel to an IKEA store that is usually located on the outskirts of a city, but it also takes a lot of energy to navigate your way through the huge and often crowded store to find exactly what you want. Then, regardless of how much planning you did, you still have to take a leap of faith and hope that the furniture you selected will actually fit in your home the way you imagined.

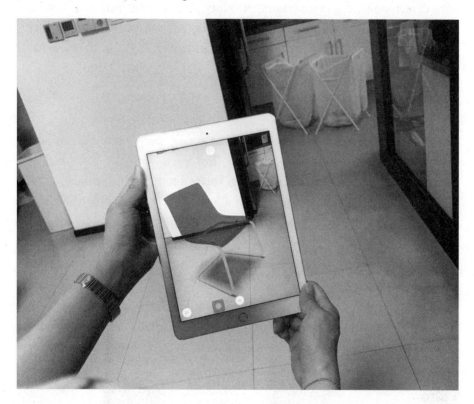

Figure 7.18. The IKEA augmented reality app. Photo credit: Amy Hsu

Johannes Ferber, a managing director for IKEA, says, "There are many city dwellers who don't have a car or aren't willing to drive outside the city to do their shopping."[48] IKEA's own research has shown that almost "14 percent of its customers end up taking home furniture which turns out to be the wrong size for its intended location."[49] To make matters worse, IKEA faces the barrier of heavily congested roadways and a lack of infrastructure in many developing markets like India, where there is also strong resistance to carrying heavy, flat-packed furniture back home to assemble on your own.

So IKEA is now using the latest AR technology to help lower purchase barriers. IKEA's new catalogue app has more than two thousand products that can be virtually placed into scanned photos of any room using AR.

Consumers no longer have to take a long journey to a store just to measure dimensions, compare colors, and buy pieces of furniture on faith before seeing what it looks like in their homes. Now users can see the furniture, place an order, and schedule delivery and assembly all with one iPhone or iPad application (see Figure 7.18).

Virtual Reality

Aaron Luber, head of VR Partnerships at Google, said, "Film used to be the most immersive storytelling medium. But even with the best, highest-resolution TVs, you're still just watching. You're not there. The promise of VR is what the industry calls 'presence'—the feeling that you're really somewhere else."[50]

Virtual reality (VR) technology creates a three-dimensional computer simulation where users can explore a virtual environment as if they were really there. The technology has advanced to the point where it has become feasible for use in mainstream applications.

In the same way that AR can help consumers in new markets "try" things before buying, VR can help consumers in new markets "experience" brands in a way that would have been very difficult or nearly impossible in the past.

Patrón

Patrón, the leading ultra-premium tequila brand in the world, now offers users a virtual tour of its hacienda in Mexico where the famous blue agave is distilled. All you need is a tablet, laptop, or Google Cardboard, and you can experience the handcrafted process that goes into making Patrón tequila and explore the hacienda's vast agave fields and surrounding landscape (see Figure 7.19).[51]

Figure 7.19. Patrón's virtual hacienda tour. Photo credit: Amy Hsu

Google Cardboard

Google Cardboard is an affordable and easy-to-use VR headset that you assemble yourself by combining it with a smartphone to deliver an impressive immersive experience (see Figure 7.20).

Now users even in remote areas of emerging and developing markets can experience things virtually that they would have never been able to experience before. For example, Google has created virtual expeditions for

Cardboard that allows students, no matter where they live, to visit places like the Great Wall of China, Machu Picchu, and the Great Barrier Reef.

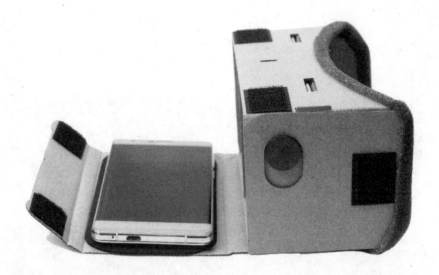

Figure 7.20. Cardboard virtual reality glasses.
Copyright: lord_photon/Bigstock

Eon Reality

I recently learned how students in Africa are now able to attend universities by using their smart mobile phones. VR technology seems like a natural next step in the evolution of mobile education.

Eon Reality is an American software brand that has created a VR platform that specializes in providing education and business solutions. Eon Reality believes that knowledge is a universal right and should be available, accessible, and affordable for every person on the planet.[52] For example, Eon is partnering with the city of Tshwane in South Africa to help instruct local students on how to create and use VR content to teach vocational skills, math, and science in local colleges.[53]

Mondly

Most language-learning experts agree that the most effective way to learn a language is through immersion. The problem is that language immersion programs are typically very expensive. For example, even the least expensive immersion option in South America will run you about $1,000 per month, effectively shutting out most emerging market students.

Romania-based ATi Studios is the owner of Mondly, the leading virtual reality language app that teaches more than thirty languages on Google's VR platforms Daydream and Cardboard. Like a real in-country immersion, Mondly recreates real-life situations and actual conversations in VR, offering instant feedback on pronunciation (see Figure 7.21). So far, there have been more than twenty million downloads in 190 countries.[54]

Figure 7.21. Mondly VR language app. Source: Mondly, with permission

Artificial Intelligence (AI) and Robots

From intelligent personal assistants like Apple's Siri to Google self-driving cars, we see the signs of artificial intelligence (AI) and machine learning almost everywhere we look. Experts agree that AI will have a significant impact on developing and emerging markets. The two areas that seem to have the most promise at the moment are healthcare and farming.

Zipline

Zipline is a California-based robotics company that delivers blood and medical supplies to remote areas of Rwanda and Tanzania via autonomous drones.

In rural Africa, about two billion people lack adequate access to essential medical care due to challenging terrain and roads, according to the World Health Organization.[55] In Africa, 95 percent of roads wash out every year.[56] By riding on mobile technology, Zipline has created a step-change in the value that medical couriers provide in Africa.

To place an order with Zipline, a medical staffer needs only to send a text message. Upon receipt of the message, Zipline loads and launches a drone from one of its distribution centers. An autonomous drone then flies at speeds of up to 60 miles per hour, arriving at its destination within thirty minutes.[57]

Butterfly iQ

Access to diagnostic medical imaging in developing and emerging markets is often in short supply. Ultrasound machines are extremely helpful in obstetrics, cardiology, and cancer detection, but a traditional machine is difficult to transport and tends to be very expensive (the average machine costs more than $100,000), and requires a trained physician to read the images (see Figure 7.22).

Butterfly iQ, a US-based medical device brand, sells a handheld imaging unit that plugs directly into an iPhone and starts at less than $2,000.

What really differentiates Butterfly iQ from competitors and provides an opportunity for the company to step-change the value it offers is its AI component? Butterfly iQ updates the software using vast datasets of ultrasound images so the app can discern between good- and bad-quality images for various body parts. The iPhone display can even guide the user to scan the best spot for capturing a good image, and the software can also conduct a simple read of the scans to help determine what steps should be taken next.[58]

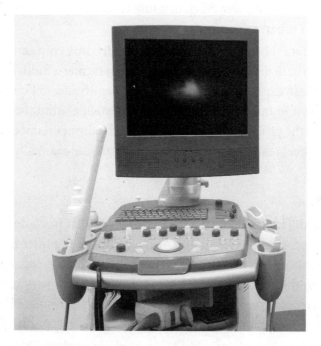

Figure 7.22. Traditional ultrasound machine.
Photo credit: uatp12/Depositphotos

Tata

The Tata group is made up of more than one hundred operating companies spread across six continents. More than 24 percent of all Internet routes travel over Tata's global communication network. Tata has invested $1.19 billion in its global fiber network, which can stretch around the world seventeen times.[59]

Vinod Kumar, MD, and CEO of Tata Communications, has spoken about the company's belief in "the transformative force that massively distributed computing and artificial intelligence can play in helping businesses get insights and solve their most complex big data problems."[60]

India is an agrarian economy with more than 58 percent of rural house-holds depending on farming as their primary source of livelihood.[61] As we touched on earlier in this chapter, farmers in developing markets need to dramatically increase their efficiency just to meet the expected growth in demand from urban migration.

Rallis, a Tata subsidiary and one of India's leading crop care companies, is using AI to help improve the yields of Indian farmers. Rallis's AI technol-ogy takes massive quantities of data on crop health and soil conditions and distills it down to information that directs pesticide-administering drones that improve the yield of crops.[62] In addition, the drones reduce the negative health side effects that come from spaying pesticides manually.

Microsoft

Microsoft India has developed an AI sowing app that has led to 30 percent higher yields. Dr. Sushas Wani, the Asia Director of the International Crop Research Institute for the Semi-Arid Tropics (ICRISAT), collaborated with Microsoft on the app and said, "Sowing date as such is very critical to en-sure that farmers harvest a good crop. And if it fails, it results in loss, as a lot of costs are incurred for seeds, as well as the fertilizer applications."[63]

To help farmers, Microsoft's AI technology analyzes historic climate data spanning the last thirty years, and real-time rainfall and soil moisture readings and forecasts. The app then sends advisories containing essential information regarding the optimal sowing date and depth, fertilizer appli-cations, seed treatments, and more.[64]

3-D printing

This is an additive manufacturing process that creates 3-D objects guided by a computer-generated design. The 3-D printer lays down successive lay-ers of building material that join together until an object is formed.

As more building materials are being developed to work with 3-D printers and the cost of the technology becomes more affordable, the popu-larity of 3-D printing is increasing. Gartner, a leading global research and advisory company, estimates that soon, nearly 50 percent of all consumer, heavy industry, and life sciences manufacturers will be using 3-D printing to produce some parts for items they consume, sell, or service.[65]

The solutions that 3-D printing provides for developed markets (e.g., tools for lean design, rapid prototyping, and bypassing a need for critical mass) become transformational in developing markets. Developing market experts agree that there is tremendous potential for 3-D printing to create disruption, especially in the areas of housing and artificial limbs.

Winsun

As in many parts of the developing world, in China there is huge demand for affordable and safe housing as a growing number of rural workers relocate to cities.

Shanghai-based Winsun is a pioneer in 3-D printing technology. The company invented the first continuous 3-D printer for construction. Winsun's unique printers measure 10 meters by 6.6 meters and use a special mix of concrete, sand, and fiberglass to print walls and other components used for building housing structures in a factory. Then, workers assemble the structures using the prefabricated panels on-site.

Winsun claims that with this technology "they can save 60 percent of the materials typically needed to construct a home of the same size, build it 70 percent faster, and with 80 percent less labor. This minimizes the environmental footprint, as well as speeds up the process, greatly reducing the chance of on-site injury."[66]

In 2013, Winsun made headlines when it built its first batch of detached single-story houses. The company constructed ten houses in less than twenty-four hours at a cost of $5,000 each (see Figure 7.23).[67]

Recently, Winsun signed an agreement to collaborate with Aecom, an American engineering firm, to help build 1.5 million affordable homes in Saudi Arabia. Yihe Ma, the chairman of WinSun, said, "This collaboration will enable us to further accelerate the development of our construction 3-D printing technology and help drive the integration of construction 3-D printing technology with planning and design."[68]

Figure 7.23. The inside of a 3-D printed home.
Photo credit: Matjazz/Shutterstock

Nia Technologies

The World Health Organization (WHO) estimates that about thirty million people require prosthetic limbs, braces, or other mobility devices. Unfortunately, fewer than two out of ten people who need mobility devices have them.[69] Nia Technologies, a Canadian nonprofit social enterprise, has developed a technology platform called PrintAbility, which is described as a digital toolchain that combines 3-D scanning, modeling, and printing with custom software and affordable hardware to produce prosthetic devices.[70]

Nia is working with Google to build an open source digital platform for orthopedic technologists—a digital "toolkit" that mirrors the manual prosthetic development process in a digital environment. Instead of creating a cast with plaster, the residual limb is scanned to create a digital model (see Figure 7.24).

Then, a 3-D model is customized to fit the patient, and a prosthetic limb can be printed in about six hours.

This digitally assisted process results in faster production times, increased access to care, better fitting devices, and shorter hospital stays, all at a cost savings to the patient.

Figure 7.24. A prosthetic socket being oriented with PrintAbility technology.
Photo credit: Nia Technologies

By leveraging 3-D printing, PrintAbility has enabled orthopedic clinicians in developing countries such as Uganda, Cambodia, and Tanzania to step-change their productivity by 333 percent and improve the lives of many young patients in those countries.[71]

Plan Your Attack

1. Identify emerging technologies that can be used to step-change your brand's growth trajectory.

2. Examine each link in your value chain to find opportunities to use technology to exceed stakeholder expectations.

3. Take advantage of existing technology that has reached a tipping point to increase your visibility of end-users and unlock demand.

Make It Happen 8

"Some people want it to happen, some wish it would happen, others make it happen."
–Michael Jordan

Illustration credit: Drawlab19/Shutterstock

Global brand builders are pioneers, forging paths into new territories to build the foundation for strong brands to grow. Long-term success is ultimately judged by the ability to create high-functioning, motivated teams—teams that are inspired to build something bigger than themselves and bring your strategy to life on the ground.

Sun Tzu wrote *Art of War* during the 5th century BC during a time of constant battles, upheaval, and uncertainty. One of Sun Tzu's famous quotes about how to win in battle reads, "He will win whose army is animated by the same spirit throughout all its ranks."[1] The implication for global brand builders is that we can't forget the needs of our teams and what motivates them as we work on satisfying the needs of our consumers.

Team Spirit

I began my marketing career at General Mills as an assistant brand manager working on adult breakfast cereals in North America. At that time, the brands I managed were all well established. Looking back, it seems strange how little I actually interacted with the sales team. Back then, brand managers at traditional CPG companies often worked in silos, developing marketing plans and products that sales teams would then be responsible for pitching to retailers. Later, I came to realize that this way of working was only made possible because General Mills had an established, well-defined structure for managing domestic brands.

When I started my first assignment overseas, I found that those systems and guardrails didn't exist anymore. There were no routine things being done on a routine basis. Because I was launching new brands into new categories in developing markets, the teams I managed didn't have the same contextual experience, and the environment we were operating in was completely different. As a result, I found I needed to work much closer with my cross-functional teammates.

Along the way, I learned that you can have the best product performance, with the best positioning, at the best price, but if your cross-functional team doesn't truly understand your brand, you will fail. That means that marketing, sales, finance, and product development all need to be on the same page. Additionally, in international environments, your stakeholders can be very diverse, which makes it necessary to keep your communication simple and easy to understand.

Make Your Communication Inspirational and Strategic

Before your message can inspire and rally your team to execute, your message needs to be on strategy, memorable, and presented in a format that can be easily adapted to ensure it remains relevant for local audiences (see Figure 8.1).

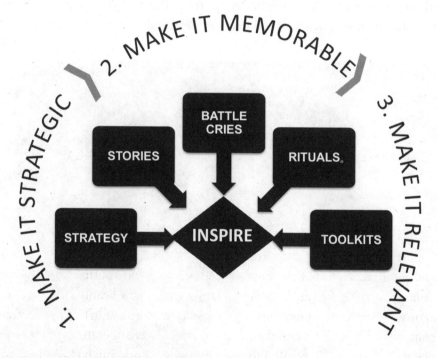

Figure 8.1. Inspirational communication framework.

When you want your brand to be understood, simply using plain language and vocabulary is not enough to get the job done. To ensure relevancy, make sure your communication is strategically grounded.

I recommend using the *Target, Key Insight, Positioning,* and *Reason to Believe* sections of the Lean Brand Canvas (see Figure 4.5 on page 61) as a communication brief. Then, evaluate your proposed communication against the "brief" to make sure your message is on strategy.

Target Consumer

Your brand's stakeholders will eventually need to become advocates for your brand, because when you send them out into the world to inspire others, it's their version of the brand story that needs to connect with the end-users. So, make sure everyone on your team clearly understands the target. A good way to accomplish this is to ground your brand story by acknowledging who your target audience is up front. This will also help your target audience believe that the brand really understands them.

Figure 8.2. Moleskine Chinese artist special edition on display at a Moleskine store in China. Photo credit: Amy Hsu

Moleskine is an Italian brand that positions its popular notebooks as a platform for creativity and often collaborates with well-known creative personalities to reinforce its positioning (see Figure 8.2 on page 206). Moleskine begins its brand story by connecting the brand with artists and thinkers.

The Moleskine brand was created in 1997, bringing back to life the legendary notebook used by artists and thinkers throughout the past two centuries, such as Vincent van Gogh, Pablo Picasso, Ernest Hemingway, and Bruce Chatwin.[2]

HSBC is one of the leading international banking and financial services organizations in the world. For years, the brand called itself "The world's local bank" (see Figure 8.3). More recently, it has focused on a message of helping customers from all over the world "realize their ambitions." HSBC begins its brand story by immediately talking about its international customers.

HSBC was born from one simple idea: a local bank serving international needs. In March 1865, HSBC opened its doors for business in Hong Kong, and today they serve around thirty-eight million customers worldwide in sixty-seven countries and territories.[3]

Figure 8.3. HSBC outdoor advertisement in Hong Kong.
Photo credit: winhorse/iStock by Getty Images

Key Insights

The brands we love change our lives for the better. However, for a brand to actually change lives, it needs to address real perceptions and problems consumers face. When using the Lean Brand Canvas, the term "key insights" includes *accepted consumer beliefs* (ACB)—genuine consumer perceptions of which brand builders can take advantage when creating solutions.

Figure 8.4. Tesla Model X. Copyright: Franz1212 | Dreamstime

Tesla is disrupting the automobile industry with cars that are simultaneously fast, sexy, and eco-friendly. The brand surprises consumers by leveraging an accepted consumer belief that electric cars must be boring to drive. Tesla is able to break through the competitive noise by surprising drivers. When you drive a Tesla, you don't have to compromise. You can own an eco-friendly vehicle that is both gorgeous and fun to drive. A survey by Gold Eagle Automotive Supplies asked two thousand people in the United States to reveal their dream car. The survey results showed the number-one choice for men and Millennials was Tesla.[4] Tesla's Model 3 won *Automobile Magazine*'s 2018 Design of the Year award. According to Robert Cumberford, the magazine's automotive design editor, "The Model 3 reminds us of classic Pininfarina designs of the 1960s: simple and straightforward, perfectly proportioned with minimal extraneous detailing" (see Figure 8.4 on page 208).[5]

In-N-Out Burger is an American west-coast-based burger chain known for its quality. You won't find any freezers, heat lamps, or microwaves in the stores. In-N-Out butchers its own beef, bakes its own buns, and only makes burgers, fries, and shakes (see Figure 8.5). The brand leverages an accepted consumer belief that burgers made the "old-fashioned way" are better than today's fast-food burgers. This strategy has worked extremely well. In-N-Out consistently ranks as one of the best regional burger chains in America.

Figure 8.5. In-N-Out Burger shop in Southern California.
Photo credit: Michael Gordon | Dreamstime

Red Bull is an Austrian beverage brand and maker of the world's leading energy drink. With its omnichannel marketing campaigns, the brand has become closely associated with extreme sports and physical activity (see Figure 8.6). Red Bull kick-started the energy drink category by leveraging a key consumer insight and accepted consumer belief: highly active people are always searching for an edge and desire something more exciting than drinking a cup of coffee to get more energy.

Figure 8.6. Red Bull rider with Red Bull helmet.
Photo credit: Stock Photo Astur/iStock by Getty Images

Brand Positioning

Your brand positioning will fundamentally determine whether consumers perceive your brand to be different from your competitors. This point of difference in the minds of consumers is what will separate your brand from other offerings that get selected primarily on price.

Rimowa is a one of Europe's leading premium travel luggage brands. The brand occupies a space that intersects the promise of luxury and precision design (see Figure 8.7).

Known for its quality construction and stylish appearance, Rimowa's grooved aluminum luggage has become an iconic design. By comparison, Louis Vuitton is a pure luxury fashion brand, focusing on fashion and heritage instead of precision engineering (see Figure 8.8).

Figure 8.7. Rimowa store window in Elements Shopping Mall, Hong Kong. Photo credit: Tea | Dreamstime

Figure 8.8. Louis Vuitton storefront in Shanghai. Photo credit: Amy Hsu

Persol is a premium Italian eyewear brand that is famous around the world for its stylishly designed sunglasses. The brand occupies the intersection between Italian design and high quality. Persol got its start by making highly functional optics for Italian pilots and sports car drivers. Later, the Italian brand became intertwined with European fashion and pop culture as celebrities began wearing Persols on film sets and in their everyday lives (see Figure 8.9).

Figure 8.9. Famous Italian actor Marcello Mastroianni wearing Persol sunglasses on a billboard. Photo credit: Arthur R./Shutterstock

Ray-Ban, on the other hand, is the quintessential American sunglass brand that got its start by making glasses for American military pilots and then offered similar designs to the general public. Hollywood thoroughly embraced the all-American positioning. You can see Ray-Ban sunglasses prominently featured in Hollywood movies such as *Risky Business, Top Gun, Blues Brothers,* and *Men in Black,* just to name a few. The American image that Ray-Ban promoted even extended into the American White House. President John F. Kennedy loved wearing his Ray-Bans almost anytime he was outdoors (see Figure 8.10).

Figure 8.10. President John F. Kennedy wearing Ray-Bans. Photo credit: Cecil Stoughton. Public Domain White House Photographs. John F. Kennedy Presidential Library and Museum, Boston

Blue Bottle Coffee Company is a "third wave" California coffee roaster and retailer specializing in single origin coffee. During the first coffee wave, the category expanded as consumers responded to the convenience of instant and percolated coffee.[6] In the second wave, big chains like Starbucks and Costa made high-quality coffee accessible to the masses[7] (see Figure 8.11). Now, in the third wave, there are new offerings like Blue Bottle Coffee Company that focus on unlocking the true flavor of the coffee bean (see Figure 8.12). Founded in 2002, Blue Bottle Coffee Company now operates more than fifty stores in the United States and Asia.

Figure 8.11. Starbucks "We belong together."
Photo credit: AppleZoomZoom/Shutterstock

Figure 8.12. A barista brewing coffee at Blue Bottle.
Photo credit: Joshua Rainey | Dreamstime

Reason to Believe

When a brand promises something, consumers want to know why they should believe the brand will deliver on its promise. These "reasons to believe," when crafted properly, help reduce barriers to trial and increase loyalty.

Pantene is a global shampoo brand owned by Procter & Gamble that promises consumers beautiful hair that is softer, shinier, smoother, and stronger. The brand tells consumers the reason they can believe it will deliver on its promise is because its products are formulated with Pro-V, a special blend of vitamins and other essential nutrients needed for healthy hair. Pantene often uses a graphic that depicts pro-vitamin bubbles to help reinforce this key reason to believe (see Figure 8.13).

Figure 8.13. Pro-V "Bubble" visual on a shampoo bottle.
Photo credit: Mirco Vacca/ Shutterstock

Dyson sales have doubled in the last six years.[8] Dyson's newest battery-powered cordless vacuum cleaners are selling extremely well across the world. In fact, its newest models have become the fastest selling vacuums in the company's twenty-five-year history.[9] Dyson promises that these new vacuum cleaners have the most powerful suction of any cordless vacuum available on the market. The reason to believe is attributed to Dyson's digital motor (see Figure 8.14). Dyson claims that the "Dyson digital motor spins up to 110,000rpm—five times faster than a Formula One car engine, producing up to 115 Air Watts."[10]

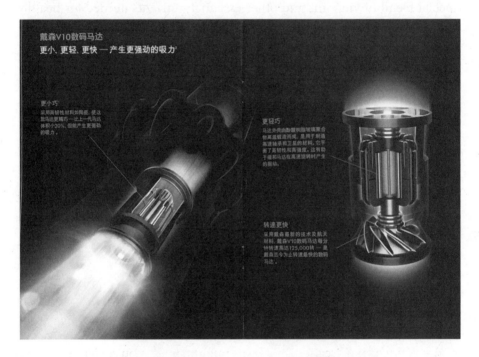

Figure 8.14. An illustration of Dyson's digital motor photographed from the China catalogue. Photo credit: Amy Hsu

Fairlife was launched in 2014 as a premium dairy brand and is distributed by The Coca-Cola Company in the United States. More consumers are starting to take notice of the brand because of its superior health credentials. Fairlife milk sales grew 79 percent in 2016[11] by promising consumers that its milk is not only delicious, but also has 50 percent more protein, 30 percent more calcium, and half the carbs of regular milk. In addition to that, Fairlife promises that its milk is lactose free (see Figure 8.15).[12]

The reason to believe that Fairlife can deliver on all of these promises is that the brand uses a proprietary cold, ultra-filtration process that "concentrates the best of milk's natural nutrients, like protein and calcium, while filtering out the lactose and reducing the sugars."[13]

Regular / Organic Whole Milk per Box	VS.	"fairlife" whole per 8oz
8g	PROTEIN	13g
280mg	CALCIUM	370mg
12g	SUGAR	6g
NO	LACTOSE FREE	YES
150	CALORIES	150
8g	FAT	8g

Figure 8.15. Fairlife comparison to whole milk.
Photo credit: Keith Homan/Shutterstock

Make It Memorable

Once your communication strategy is put into place, you can craft a memorable narrative that includes a brand story and supporting mechanics like brand rituals and a "battle cry" to make sure your story is engaging and easy to remember.

Tell a Story

Telling a story helps us connect and bond with others. Research shows that we empathize and remember more information when it's conveyed in a story format.[14]

Think about your own engagement level when information is presented as a list of facts versus when someone tells you a story. Jeremy Donovan, author of *How to Deliver a TED Talk* teaches people how to give presentations and writes, "Every idea worth spreading must be packaged in a story worth telling."[15] One of the reasons that I enjoy watching TED Talks so much is because when good speakers share their stories, it can sometimes feel like you are right there in the story with them.

It turns out that our preference for hearing stories is hardwired into our brains and the result of our human evolution. Before humans could write, we told each other stories to convey important information and make sure our messages would be remembered.

A study at Princeton University found that when we hear well-crafted stories, our brains react as if we were actually participating in the story. This is also true for the storyteller.[16] When researchers studied MRI scans of people telling and listening to stories, they found that brain activity for both recipients and presenters mirrored each other, helping to explain that magical feeling of connection that can happen when you are listening to a good story.[17]

Meet the Critical Objectives of a Brand Story

Brand stories are so important, which is why brand builders need guidance on how to craft a good one. Whenever I coach brand managers on how to write an engaging narrative, I encourage them to use the following framework to evaluate a story based on its ability to meet the following three critical objectives: 1) break through the noise; 2) sustain interest; and 3) generate empathy (see Figure 8.16).

- **Break through the noise:** First, every brand story needs to break through and grab the listener's attention before anything else. If a consumer isn't paying attention, your story is never going to be heard.

- **Sustain interest:** After you get the consumer's attention, you need to keep it. The brand story needs to sustain that attention. You do this by creating suspense, using vivid language, and incorporating visuals that make your story feel more authentic. If the story is not rooted in truth, your consumers will sense it and think your story is just advertising.

♦ **Generate empathy:** It is very important that you make sure your story contains emotional content. When listeners empathize with your story, they will remember it. In his book *Brain Rules,* molecular biologist John Medina says that when a brain is exposed to emotionally charged content, the amygdala releases dopamine into the body. Besides making you feel good, dopamine helps with memory and information processing. "You could say it creates a Post-It note that reads, 'Remember this.'"[18]

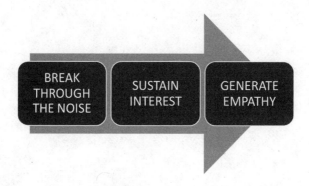

Figure 8.16. Brand story framework.

Consumers and stakeholders also become more engaged with a story when they believe a brand truly understands them. Consumers want to trust that a brand knows what it feels like to walk in their shoes. In fact, research shows that empathy is very important for stakeholders. Eighty-two percent of employees believe that empathy is a key way to influence.[19]

The TOMS Story

While traveling in Argentina in 2006, TOMS founder Blake Mycoskie witnessed the hardships faced by children growing up without shoes. Wanting to help, he created TOMS Shoes.

TOMS is a for-profit brand, headquartered in California. The company is known around the world for its One for One business model in which it gives a pair of free shoes to a child in need for every pair of shoes sold in retail.[20] TOMS brand story instantly grabs the listener's attention and begins to encourage empathy by focusing on children from developing countries who can't afford to wear shoes. The story feels authentic, and on its website, the brand includes pictures of its founder, Blake Mycoskie, giving shoes away to poor children in Argentina (see Figure 8.17).

Figure 8.17. TOMS founder Blake Mycoskie. Photo credit: Andy Sternberg

Burt's Bees

Burt and Roxanne hit it off. From those first candles to the iconic beeswax lip balm we all know today, Burt's Bees has stayed true to a very simple idea: what you put on your body should be made from the best nature has to offer.[21]

Burt's Bees is an American brand that helped pioneer natural personal care and embraced the concept of sustainability before the word was commonly used (see Figure 8.18).[22] The Burt's Bees brand story does a great job of creating and sustaining interest by sharing the true but surprising story about how a large brand got its humble start. The brand's website incorporates old photographs of the founders, which reinforces the brand's positioning by reminding people of a time when things were simpler and more natural.

Figure 8.18. An example of Burt's Bees packaging.
Photo credit: Keith Homan/Shutterstock

CLIF Bar

"CLIF Bar is named after my father, Clifford, my childhood hero . . . the inspiration to create an energy bar occurred during a 175-mile bike ride. We'd been gnawing on some other energy bars all day. Suddenly, despite my hunger, I couldn't take another bite. I thought, 'I could make a better bar than this!'"[23]

CLIF Bar is an American health and lifestyle brand that began as an alternative to traditional energy bars. The brand now sells more than a dozen product lines and exports to eighteen different countries throughout Europe, Asia, and Australia.[24] The CLIF bar brand story starts with an emotional punch as Gary (the founder) discusses his relationship with his father, whom he calls his hero. Then the story introduces the moment when Gary had his epiphany that inspired all his work. Gary takes the listener on a journey from his garage to creating a better-tasting energy bar out of his mom's kitchen. The brand's website includes a great picture of Gary and his dad, which helps communicate the brand's authenticity and facilitates message recall.

Johnnie Walker

John Walker's father had just died. No time to grieve. There was a living to be made. John had a genius for whisky. Most grocers stocked single malts, but they were never consistent. This wasn't good enough for John, who started blending them together so his whisky tasted just as good every time.[25]

Johnnie Walker is the most widely distributed blended Scotch Whisky in the world, sold in over two hundred countries.[26] The Johnnie Walker brand story is made more powerful by creating synergy between the brand's "Striding Man" logo and battle cry "Keep Walking."

According to Diageo, the logo and battle cry both communicate the concept of marching forward toward progress and the fulfillment of personal goals (see Figure 8.19 on the following page).[27] You can feel this concept come to life in the brand story.

Figure 8.19. Johnnie Walker whisky Striding Man monument statue.
Photo credit: Boreccy | Dreamstime

The brand story immediately gets your attention with a death and then sustains it by creating suspense as the listener waits to hear how John Walker will lift himself up and "Keep Walking." The brand amplifies this key association by using the "journey" metaphor that originates from the brand story to frame other real stories of achievement from its brand ambassadors and customers, resulting in increased engagement and loyalty for the brand.

Sound Bites

I often hear people complain about how the news media only speaks in sound bites, making it difficult to comprehend the complete story. That may be true, but in international marketing, well-crafted sound bites are not only needed, they are also highly effective.

I know it is a cliché, but things too often get lost in translation—even between people who speak the same language. Creating brand communication in a "sound bite" format forces the writer to crystalize the brand message. Then, stakeholders can take those "golden nuggets" and integrate them into their conversations with the wider brand community.

The collection of sound bites that you provide to your sales team and other stakeholders should not be limited to product performance. Brands are continuously renovating and improving, so precise performance claims need to be constantly updated. However, the heart of your brand and its reason for being should remain consistent over time.

Battle Cries

Battle cries like Johnnie Walker's "Keep Walking" can evoke real emotion and inspire stakeholders to take action. In business, as in war, battle cries can have a unifying effect, which provide an encapsulation of a brand's ethos and act as a compass that guides the team in a common direction and informs customers of what they can expect.

When I worked on the DaVinci Gourmet brand, I led the creation of the battle cry "Flavor Genius." It is very effective because the "cry" is connected to the actual inspiration for the brand, Leonardo da Vinci, who was a genius. The slogan also encapsulates the brand's promise of helping professional drink makers create their own drink masterpieces.

The phrase is very popular within the extended brand community. It became a unifying mechanism among a group of diverse brand stakeholders due to its simplicity and how it applies to both the brand's expertise and the customers who aspire to be flavor geniuses (see Figure 8.20).

Powerful battle cries have the following elements:

+ They are simple and easy to remember.
+ They evoke emotion.
+ They communicate the brand's reason for being.

The following examples are extremely powerful battle cries from two of the world's most successful brands.

Figure 8.20. DaVinci Gourmet website landing page.
Source: DaVinci Gourmet, used with permission

Walmart

Walmart is the world's largest retail chain, hiring roughly 2.3 million workers in more than eleven thousand stores across twenty-eight countries.[28] Judith McKenna, the CEO of Walmart International, says you can ask any of her associates why Walmart exists, and they should be able to recite the company's battle cry, "We save people money, so they can live better."[29] It's a simplified version of the company's mission statement and also shows up in the brand's advertising slogan, "Save Money. Live Better." (see Figure 8.21).

Figure 8.21. Walmart sign with simplified version of the company battle cry.
Photo credit: Snyfer | Dreamstime

The company's battle cry is not only easy to remember and understand, but it also captures the driving force behind everything that Walmart does and asks employees and stakeholders to do for the greater good. It evokes real emotion, in part, because it is based on what Sam Walton, the company's founder, actually believed. Sam famously said, "If we work together, we'll lower the cost of living for everyone . . . we'll give the world an opportunity to see what it's like to save and have a better life."[30]

Apple

In 1997, Apple launched its "Think Different" slogan and campaign. As Steve Jobs was introducing the new campaign to a group of Apple employees, he spoke about how the campaign captured what Apple stood for and how the brand fit into the world. This is how he described Apple's core value:

> What we're about isn't making boxes for people to get their jobs done, though we do that well. We do that better than almost anybody in some cases. But Apple's about something more than that: Apple, at the core, its core value, is we believe that people with passion can change the world for the better. That's what we believe.[31]

The Think Different advertising campaign was launched with a television ad called "Here's to the Crazy Ones," featuring an impressive collection of creative visionaries, such as Albert Einstein, Bob Dylan, Martin Luther King, John Lennon, Thomas Edison, Muhammad Ali, Gandhi, Alfred Hitchcock, and Pablo Picasso. Black-and-white images of the visionary thinkers were shown and a manifesto was read by actor Richard Dreyfuss:

> Here's to the crazy ones. The misfits. The rebels. The troublemakers. The round pegs in the square holes. The ones who see things differently. They're not fond of rules. And they have no respect for the status quo. You can quote them, disagree with them, glorify or vilify them. About the only thing you can't do is ignore them. Because they change things. They invent. They imagine. They heal. They explore. They create. They inspire. They push the human race forward. Maybe they have to be crazy. How else can you stare at an empty

canvas and see a work of art? Or sit in silence and hear a song that's never been written? Or gaze at a red planet and see a laboratory on wheels? We make tools for these kinds of people. While some see them as the crazy ones, we see genius. Because the people who are crazy enough to think they can change the world, are the ones who do.[32]

Images of the visionary thinkers were also used in print and outdoor media to reinforce the message (see Figure 8.22).

"Think Different" went on to become a battle cry for Apple that was still used twenty years later. It is simple and easy to remember, and inspires people inside and outside the company, while communicating Apple's reason for being. Steve Jobs said, "Think Different represented what the brand was all about and touched the soul of the company."[33]

Figure 8.22. Apple "Think Different" billboard advertisement.
Photo credit: Gilles Mingasson/Getty Images

Brand Rituals

Japanese culture is well known for the importance placed on rituals. Ancient ninjas practiced a ritual made up of nine hand gestures called Kuji-Kiri (see Figure 8.23). These gestures were used to help them focus energy and, in some cases, inspire enlightenment. Kuji-Kiri worked by helping a ninja focus on a set of ideas and concepts stored in memory, giving him the spiritual and psychological tools to accomplish a mission.[34]

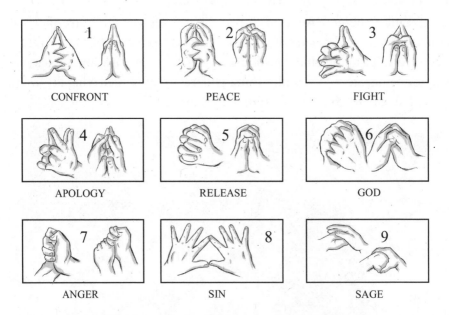

Figure 8.23. Kuji-Kiri hand ritual gestures. Source: John 062

Rituals also help global brands expanding into new markets by

♦ Reinforcing what the brand stands for in the minds of stakeholders.

♦ Encouraging participants to bond with the wider user group and brand.

♦ Motivating team performance and inspiring growth.

♦ Encouraging frequency and usage.

Research shows that people enjoy performing a task more when it's combined with a ritual. In fact, when people perform a ritual, they become more invested and, as a result, feel better regardless of the outcome.[35]

Brands like Oreo cookies and Reese's peanut butter cups have long known that rituals can make food taste better, which is why both brands encourage consumers to create their own consumption rituals (see Figures 8.24 and 8.25).

Figure 8.24. Oreo's twist, lick, dunk iPhone app. Photo credit: Amy Hsu

Figure 8.25. How do you eat your Reese's? Photo credit: Amy Hsu

In one research study, respondents were asked to eat a chocolate bar. Half were told to perform a ritual that included breaking and unwrapping the bar in a specific way before eating it. The other half were allowed to eat the chocolate bar anyway they wanted. The results showed that on average, those who performed the ritual enjoyed eating the candy more and also thought the chocolate was worth more.[36]

Clinique

Clinique was the first dermatologist-tested brand to be sold globally.[37] In 1968, Clinique introduced a simple 3-step skincare ritual with accompanying facial products: Step 1 Cleanse, Step 2 Exfoliate, and Step 3 Moisturize.

When you visit a Clinique cosmetic counter, a consultant will likely encourage you to schedule a free makeover that begins with its famous 3-step skincare ritual (see Figure 8.26). The ritual not only helps standardize the way the brand consultants engage with consumers, but also makes it easier for associates to sell.

Figure 8.26. Clinique 3-step skincare line display. Photo credit: Amy Hsu

As consumers use the product at home, the 3-step skincare process often becomes a ritual that fans claim they look forward to completing each day, leading to an increase in brand loyalty and a stronger connection with the brand.

That's why Clinique aggressively distributes free samples of its 3-step skincare line at its cosmetic counters all over the world in hopes of having the ritual take hold (see Figure 8.27). Psychological research published in the *European Journal of Social Psychology* found on average it takes about one and a half months for a ritual to become a habit.[38]

Figure 8.27. Clinique 3-step free sample sachets. Photo credit: Amy Hsu

Stella Artois

Stella Artois is one of the oldest brands in the world, first appearing in 1336.[39] The percentage of alcohol content in Stella Artois is 5.2 percent a bit higher than the 4.7 percent average found in other lagers.

In the 1990s, the brand's image was suffering as consumers began to perceive that Stella Artois was the beer of choice for football hooligans and binge drinkers, in part due to its high alcohol content and discount pricing.

In 2008, the brand launched a lower alcohol content lager and used the occasion as an opportunity to refresh the brand's positioning. That's when the brand introduced its famous "9-step pouring ritual" and created a new "glass chalice." When a bartender follows the 9-step ritual, it ensures the proper skill and precision are used when pouring a pint of Stella Artois (see Figure 8.28).[40]

To encourage adoption of the ritual in the trade, Stella Artois sponsors Draught Master competitions all over the world during which bartenders get to express their passion for the beer and show off their 9-step pouring ritual.[41] Currently, Stella Artois is one of the world's fastest growing beer brands.[42]

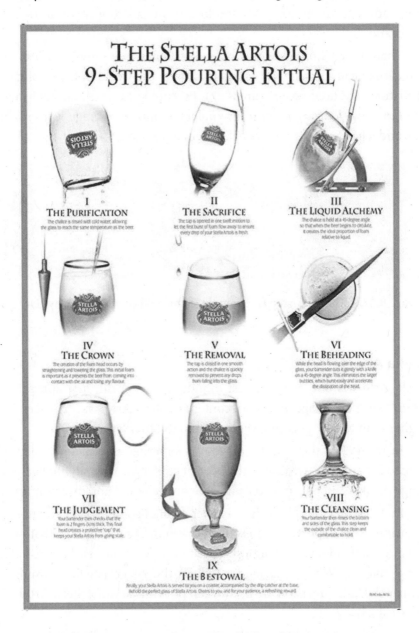

Figure 8.28. Stella Artois 9-step pouring ritual printed on a poster.
Photo credit: Rik Thompson

Corona Extra

Corona Extra arrived in the United States in 1981 and is now the most popular beer import in America.[43] You have probably noticed that anytime you see a Corona in an advertisement or at a bar, the bottle will almost always have a lime wedge stuck into the neck. There are many stories for how this ritual came about. Some people swear that the ritual began as a way to sanitize the opening of Corona's not-so-clean-looking recycled beer bottles that came from Mexico, or that the lime was used to repel flies. I find the most credible reason is that American consumers enjoyed performing the ritual and believed that it made their beers taste better.

Figure 8.29. Corona advertisement.
Photo credit by venge.mail.ua/Depositphotos

It is said that when Grupo Modelo, the producer of Corona Extra, began noticing that Americans were shoving lime wedges into their Corona bottles, the company was not actually happy about it. The American habit was making the bottles more difficult to recycle and increasing costs. However, when the company realized how much sales were being generated as a result of the ritual, it not only accepted it, but began promoting Coronas with limes in all of the brand communication (see Figure 8.29 on page 233).[44] This ritual is generally credited with helping Corona overtake Heineken as the bestselling imported beer in the US market.[45]

Make It Relevant

As Peter Drucker said, "Strategy is a commodity, execution is an art."[46] So for us global brand builders, it all comes down to execution. If your stakeholders cannot bring your brand positioning and value proposition to life on the ground, your brand will never become relevant to consumers. To bring the brand to life, stakeholders require a clear understanding of the brand, what's in and what's out, what elements of the brand strategy can be adapted, and which must remain constant.

Create a Brand Toolkit

The best global brand builders I know create digital toolkits designed to meet the needs of lead markets and their corresponding satellite cities. A brand toolkit should include style guides, adaptable media templates, "springboard" content, sales/training materials, and approved brand assets and visuals. The materials should all be placed on a digital cloud platform that can be easily accessed by local stakeholders and then customized to satisfy local audiences.

Danone

Danone uses the digital toolkit approach to help manage the differences in consumer needs between international markets. Global marketing teams create brand frameworks and global strategies that local markets can then adapt to meet local needs. Olivia Sanchez, vice president of marketing for Evian at Danone, says these toolkits ensure "the look and feel. What the local markets provide is the context and they ensure that it's appropriate for each market."[47]

Unilever

Fifty-seven percent of Unilever's sales are derived from emerging markets.[48] In 2013, Unilever began testing a digital content management system with Percolate, a global content marketing platform. The system included an image editor and a media management solution to help the company's central marketing team increase the visual quality and consistency of its local execution.

As a result of using this platform, Unilever was able to enforce stronger brand guidelines and increase efficiencies that resulted in less time spent on creating and approving content while decreasing the cost of content creation. Unilever and Percolate estimate that using this platform generates an annual savings of more than $10 million.[49]

Coca-Cola

Coca-Cola uses a centralized structure to guide content creation and execution at the local market level. Coca-Cola's social media hub is located in Atlanta, Georgia, and supports a network of more than twenty regional information centers globally. The network manages social media marketing for Coca-Cola's trademarked brands, supporting more than two thousand global marketers around the world.[50]

The social media hub is staffed by more than fifty-five people, including marketing and agency partners who are listening to and analyzing social conversations from around the world. These experts take what they are hearing and use it to develop content strategy, media content, and manage online communities and media buys.[51] The hub is also responsible for creating digital toolkits that contain adaptable content for specific sales channels.

For example, to increase consumer engagement for its Freestyle dispenser on Facebook, Instagram, and Twitter, Coca-Cola created a foodservice channel toolkit. The toolkit contains "copy and imagery examples for promotions, specialty drinks, time-sensitive content, limited-time offers, mixing ideas, and restaurant openings. It also includes insights on optimizing post visibility (making sure your posts get seen) and responsive messaging (replying to customers who comment on your posts), as well as links to share with followers and instructions for accessing Coca-Cola Freestyle logos and imagery" so foodservice operators can create fun, engaging content easily.[52]

Plan Your Attack

1. Use the Lean Brand Canvas to help you capture your brand strategy in an easy-to-communicate format.

2. Create a brand story that 1) creates breakthrough; 2) sustains interest; and 3) generates empathy.

3. Augment your brand story with sound bites, rituals, and a "rally cry" to help increase comprehension and engagement.

Get Creative 9

"*Creative thinking 'in terms of idea creativity' is not a mystical talent. It is a skill that can be practiced and nurtured.*"
–Edward de Bono

"*You have to follow your intuitive nature.*"
–Phil Jackson

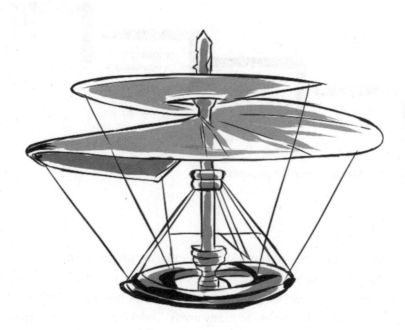

When launching a new brand into an emerging or developing market, you need the freedom to adapt and think outside the box—to get creative. The game-changing ideas that transform organizations and unlock growth are born out of creativity, and that creativity is always built on and judged against existing knowledge.

Merge Your Intuition with Analysis

I was drawn to brand marketing because of a perception that marketing organizations value creativity. I always had good intuition but learned early on in my career that I needed to merge my intuition with analysis in order to get stakeholders to follow my lead. So, I developed and continue to use a *merged creative process* with all my teams to encourage innovative thinking that can result in step-change growth (see Figure 9.1).

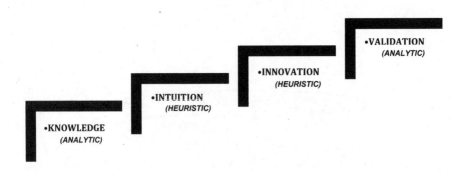

Figure 9.1. Merged creative process.

Knowledge

Knowledge is the first step in a merged creative process. Think about the most creative people you know, the ones who come up with innovative solutions that actually work. Chances are they're not just experts in one field but extremely knowledgeable in many areas. That's because creativity needs a springboard of knowledge to jump off from.

Consider creative geniuses like da Vinci, Michelangelo, and Picasso. They began their formal training by learning about and emulating the masters. Da Vinci worked for years as an assistant to Andrea del Verrocchio, working on small sections of Verrocchio's paintings before eventually ascending to the level of a master himself. Michelangelo started by studying and copying paintings in churches, while Picasso began his journey by interpreting the styles of the Old Masters, but managing to add his own little twist. Picasso later said, "Good artists borrow, great artists steal."[1]

The journey to becoming a master brand builder or a brand ninja begins with observing and gathering knowledge (Know Yourself, Know Your Enemy) and culminates in creativity. That's why I intentionally waited until the end of the book to tackle the important role that creativity plays in building strong global brands.

I recommend developing a personalized system for continuous learning and then encouraging your team members to do the same. Make it a habit to read more. Socio-economist Randall Bell has studied the core characteristics of great achievers for the past twenty-five years. In his book *Me We Do Be*, he writes, "Those who read seven or more books per year are 122 percent more likely to become millionaires as opposed to those who never read or only read one to three [books]."[2] Elon Musk is a great example, as he read up to ten hours a day growing up. Mark Cuban continues to read as much as three hours a day, while Bill Gates is known to read fifty books a year.[3] Create a learning plan with scheduled times for thinking and sharing insights with others. Broaden your perspective by establishing a cross-functional network of experts inside and outside of your work to expand your breadth of knowledge and fuel your intuition.

Creative Genius

Creativity reveals itself through new ideas that are perceived to be different from the status quo. I always tell the advertising and design agencies I work with that anyone can be creative, but "creative genius" is much more than just being creative; it's being creative while also adhering to specific constraints and requirements (e.g., operational, cultural, and financial).

I must warn you that the road to becoming a "creative" marketer can be challenging. Those who have not developed their own creative abilities often find it difficult to "connect the dots." For them, creative solutions seem inherently riskier because they are derived in part through intuition.

Intuition

Intuition is the second step in the merged creative process after you have observed and gathered knowledge (see Figure 9.1 on page 238). Unlike the act of studying, which is a conscious, analytical process, intuition operates in the subconscious mind. Nevertheless, you can greatly improve the accuracy of your intuition just by consciously acquiring relevant knowledge and experience.

Most new products fail because innovation is not easy. Creative solutions cannot be calculated using a strict formula. Daniel Pink, the author of *Drive*, gets it right when he says that creative solutions are not algorithmic (following a set path), but rather heuristic, breaking from the path to discover a novel strategy.[4]

That ability to see the "break" in the set path ahead is intuition. Albert Einstein wrote, "There will come a point in everyone's life, however, where only intuition can make the leap ahead, without ever knowing precisely how. One can never know why but one must accept intuition as a fact."[5]

Adjust Your Aversion to Risk

When you're managing a large existing business in a developed market, there is tremendous risk associated with any decision to do something different. On the other hand, when you're building a new brand in a developing market, you should be operating lean (e.g., co-creating rapid prototypes and using ninja-style research, resulting in significantly more upside.

Go Faster

When you are entering new markets, speed can be a competitive advantage, and your intuition can help you identify creative solutions faster.

Intuition likely evolved as a survival mechanism. Early humans struggling to survive didn't have the time to carefully weigh out all the facts before having to make life-or-death decisions.[6] Did you know that the unconscious mind can process roughly eleven million pieces of information per second, while the conscious mind only process about forty pieces per second?[7]

As we work to accumulate knowledge and experience, our unconscious mind continues to process what we have studied and saves it for future use. Brain imaging research confirms that our brains continue making calculations even when we have consciously moved on to other tasks.[8]

Elite athletes are mesmerizing to watch because their performances can feel like artistic expression, and at times appear to be superhuman. For example, Michael Jordan seemed to float over other basketball players as he made his way to the basket. Lionel Messi's speed and agility make other football (soccer) players on the pitch look like they're playing in slow motion, and Roger Federer's brilliant attacking style can leave other tennis players looking like they're continuously one step behind.

So, what do these elite athletes all have in common? Why do they always seem to put themselves at the right place, at the right time, and usually get there faster than their competitors? They are all excellent at harnessing and trusting their intuition while playing. Sports scientists call this phenomenon *coincident anticipation timing* (CAT)."[9] In other words, athletes can use their intuition to predict where the ball is going to be before the ball even gets there. My favorite example is Dennis Rodman. At only 6 foot, 7 inches, Rodman was one of the best rebounders in NBA history. He led the NBA in rebounds per game for a record seven consecutive years and won five NBA championships in the process.

Intuitively, Rodman seemed to know where the basketball was going to go before a missed shot was even taken. A major factor in his success was his extreme dedication to studying the science of basketball. Rodman would relentlessly watch game film and observe how others played. He learned how the number of rotations a ball makes affects how a ball bounces and how the angle and velocity of a shot determine its trajectory. The more Rodman learned, the more accurate his intuition became.

Innovation

The third step in the creative process is innovation. This is where you get to merge all of your acquired knowledge with your sharpened intuition to create innovative solutions. Remember: Neither pure logic nor intuition can achieve "creative genius." To achieve optimal results, you need to harness both your subconscious and conscious mind. In the creative process I have put forth, both approaches are needed; steps one and four (knowledge and validation) are analytical, whereas steps two and three (intuition and innovation) are heuristic (see Figure 9.1).

Using a merged (analytical/heuristic) approach for reaching optimal solutions is not radical thinking. In fact, many great thinkers and innovators throughout history have advocated for this type of balanced approach.

Lao Tzu

The ancient Chinese *Tao Te Ching* is attributed to philosopher Lao Tzu around 2500 BC. The book describes the philosophy of Taoism, which advocates using your intuition and knowledge to interpret the world. Lao Tzu understood that you could cultivate your intuition by simply expanding your awareness of the natural laws that govern the patterns and cycles of nature.[10] Bruce Lee famously practiced Taoism and credits the philosophy to helping him beat much larger opponents by seeing them as part of the "one." Lee once said, "Taoist philosophy is essentially monistic. Matter and energy, Yang and Yin, heaven and earth are conceived of as essentially one or as two coexistent poles of one indivisible whole."[11]

Siddhartha Gotama

The word *Buddhism* is derived from the word "buhdi," which means "to awaken." Buddhism originated about 2,500 years ago when Siddhartha Gotama, later known as the Buddha, awakened.[12] After many years of study and meditation, Siddhartha discovered a "middle path" to enlightenment. This middle way avoids extremes, resulting in a balanced approach, being sensitive to internal thoughts, speech, and actions, while also seeking a rational understanding of the world.[13]

Leonardo da Vinci

Leonardo da Vinci is one of the fathers of the High Renaissance and is famous for using both science and art to create his masterpieces.

Walter Isaacson, author of the biography *Leonardo da Vinci,* claims that a key to da Vinci's creative genius was his amazing ability to blur the boundaries between art and science. Da Vinci was extremely observant, constantly taking notes and obsessively curious about how the world operated around him. The knowledge he accumulated gave him a "spiritual feel" for patterns of nature.[14]

Albert Einstein

It is natural to assume that Albert Einstein probably preferred logic to intuition, but the opposite is actually true. Einstein famously said, "The intuitive mind is a sacred gift and the rational mind is a faithful servant. We have created a society that honors the servant and has forgotten the gift."[15]

It is well known that Einstein actually preferred to think in images and feelings, and then translate those ideas into scientific and mathematical words and symbols. In Wertheimer's *Productive Thinking,* Einstein explains, "I rarely think in words at all. A thought comes, and I may try to express in words afterwards." In his autobiographical notes, he goes on to explain, "I have no doubt that our thinking goes on for the most part without the use of symbols, and, furthermore, largely unconsciously."[16]

Einstein once even told a friend, "When I examine myself and my methods of thought, I come close to the conclusion that the gift of imagination has meant more to me than my talent for absorbing absolute knowledge."[17]

Steve Jobs

Steve Jobs also believed in the power of intuitive thinking. He expressed discomfort with consumer research not because he didn't believe in its ability to validate ideas, but because he didn't believe consumers could tell him what the next iPhone was going to be. He once famously said, "Intuition is a very powerful thing, more powerful than intellect, in my opinion. That's had a big impact on my work."[18]

Like da Vinci, Steve Jobs loved playing in that intersection between art and science. He believed that intuition came from experience and that true art required a disciplined approach. In an interview with the Smithsonian, Jobs said, "I think the artistry is in having an insight into what one sees around them. Generally putting things together in a way no one else has before and finding a way to express that to other people who don't have that insight so they can get some of the advantage of that insight."[19]

According to Walter Isaacson, Steve Jobs's biographer, Jobs trusted his intuition to the point that he was able to connect artistry and technology to take imaginative leaps. "His whole life is a combination of mystical enlightenment thinking with hard core rational thought."[20]

Jeff Bezos

Like Steve Jobs, Jeff Bezos is another creative brand builder who doesn't depend solely on consumer surveys to give him game-changing ideas. Bezos believes in studying consumer behavior to develop intuition and insights that can then be leveraged in the creative process. In Amazon's 2016 Letter to Shareholders, he wrote,

Good inventors and designers deeply understand their customer. They study and understand many anecdotes rather than only the averages you'll find on surveys. I'm not against beta testing or surveys. But you, the product or service owner, must understand the customer, have a vision, and love the offering. Then, beta testing and research can help you find your blind spots. A remarkable customer experience starts with heart, intuition, curiosity, play, guts, taste. You won't find any of it in a survey.[21]

Creativity Hacks

After you build up a reservoir of knowledge and refine your intuition, it will be time to start generating innovative, game-changing ideas. I listed some of the "hacks" that I find to be the most productive when working on creative ideas with my teams. Feel free to expand and personalize the list based on your own creative thinking style and experience.

Empathetic Thinking

With this approach, you get to put on the end-user hat and imagine what they would want and need. UberEATS, a food-delivery app from Uber, is a good example of how a brand can benefit from using empathetic thinking to identify new solutions and opportunities. Currently operating in two hundred cities globally, UberEATS has become very successful. The service was initially rolled out in Los Angeles, New York, and Chicago, and now delivers food from more than 220,000 restaurants in more than five hundred cities globally.[22]

UberEATS invites end-users and cross-functional experts to a central location to ideate and share their experiences from similar services to generate insights and empathy for its end-users. The company credits such innovative ideas as its "pooled deliveries" and "virtual restaurants" that are available only on UberEATS to this empathetic design approach.[23]

Analogue Thinking

This approach encourages you take an idea that is working in another category or industry and redesign it to solve a new need. The Dyson vacuum cleaner is a perfect example of using an analogue thinking approach.

When James Dyson began working on a better vacuum cleaner, he purchased the "best" vacuum he could find and, in his opinion, found that it did not do a very good job of sucking up dirt, but instead just pushed it around. James remembered seeing an industrial sawmill that had a good method of removing dust from the air using a cyclonic separator. He wondered if the same principle of separation might work in a vacuum cleaner. So, he created a quick prototype and the rest is history. The Dyson vacuum became a billion-dollar business.[24]

Systems Thinking

When using systems thinking, you can begin by doing a teardown of a reference product and then recreate it, looking for new combinations and ways to improve efficiency and effectiveness. This is the creative approach that Apple used to invent the iPhone.

Recognizing that a convergence of mobile phone and MP3 technology was occurring, Apple engineers tore down existing mobile phones to understand what was working and what wasn't in an effort to build a better mobile phone. Then, they did the same thing with their own iPod design. In the end, they took the best of the iPod and put it into a phone. In fact, "The first concept for an iPhone type device came about in 2000 when Apple worker John Casey sent some concept art around via internal email. He called it the 'Telipod' a telephone and iPod combination."[25]

Springboard Thinking

With springboard thinking, you begin by collecting learning and insights on specific platforms that will later be used to "spring" from when ideating on new ideas. This "stimulus," in effect, acts as a shortcut so participants don't have to acquire an expert level of knowledge before participating in an ideation session.

Taco Bell uses this approach to prepare for its innovation sessions. According to Melissa Friebe, vice president of Taco Bell's Insights Lab, her team synthesizes data and insights across a wide range of sources, providing in-house consultation services to her cross-functional counterparts at Taco Bell.[26] Some of the platforms that Taco Bell has ideated on recently include the breakfast occasion, healthier menu options, mashups, Instagram/Twitter worthy, better value, and more flavor. Taco Bell's innovation sessions have resulted in a recent series of successful product launches that include Doritos Locos Tacos, Waffle Taco, Cheesy Core Burrito, and Nacho Fries.

Doritos Locos Tacos was conceived in a brainstorming session. If you haven't seen this product, it's a taco with a shell that's dusted in cheesy Doritos flavoring. Taco Bell sold more than a billion dollars' worth of Doritos Locos Tacos in the first twenty months after its launch.[27] The menu item incredibly delivers on more flavor, mashup, and Instagram worthiness all in one offering.

The original concept sprang from a simple question: How do you make a taco more flavorful? In an interview with QSR magazine, Friebe said, "One of the things that we hold ourselves to is that there has to be a reason why we create the product . . . whether we're looking at food culture, pop culture, or looking at conventional things and twisting them up—they're always grounded in a consumer need."[28]

Validatation

Validation is a part of the merged creative process (see Figure 9.1). Use ninja research techniques to increase your confidence level and provide direction on how to fix potential communication problems. Although consumers may not be able to tell you what the next iPhone will be, they can certainly tell you if they don't understand your concept and why.

I highly recommend using a lean process (see Figure 4.3), one that includes rapid prototyping, guerrilla research, fast learning, and pivoting. Don't be afraid to pivot to a new idea. If you determine that your idea is flawed, that is a good outcome, because it means you can safely eliminate some "white space" and focus on areas that have a higher probability for success.

Finally, validate to persuade others. Stakeholders, who are more left-brain-oriented, will want you to prove that your idea can work. Proof of concept will help you gain their trust and support. In *The Lean Startup*, Eric Ries writes, "Prove to yourself that your business, in micro-scale at least, creates value. If you believe it, you'll find it that much easier to convince potential investors, partners and employees, too."[29]

Plan Your Attack

1. Grow your knowledge especially in categories outside of your own to improve your intuition hit rate.

2. Learn to trust your intuition and merge analytical and heuristic thinking to arrive at breakthrough solutions.

3. Use "creativity hacks" to stimulate innovative thinking and problem solving.

Conclusion:
The Secret Traditions of the
Global Brand Builder

"Sometimes it's the journey that teaches you a lot about your destination."
–Drake

hope you enjoyed taking this journey with me. I tried to capture the essence of what I learned on the road to becoming a global brand builder. I also hope that you have had some fun drawing on the ninja parallels.

One the most important ninja manuals in existence is the *Shinobi Hiden* written by Hattori Hanzo around 1560 and later translated into English under the name *The Secret Traditions of the Shinobi.* Inspired by the idea of condensing the secret teachings of how to be a ninja into one manual, I named this Conclusion after the historical text.

We have covered quite a lot of material, so I thought it important to list what I believe are the key takeaways from each chapter. Feel free to use them to simply refresh your memory or to spark additional thinking and discussion.

The Ninja

+ Global brand builders must adopt a lean approach to compete with larger, slower-moving, more established competitors.

+ Both ninjas and global brand builders have an advantage in common that requires them to observe and gather knowledge and insights before engaging in a fight.

+ Asymmetric warfare necessitates identifying what ties your opponent to the status quo, helping you figure out how to take advantage of that predictability.

See the New Battleground

+ Even as an emerging consumer class and urban migration are creating more opportunities, those same forces are generating added complexity and an increased need to adapt to local consumer needs.

+ To be effective, global brand builders must be willing to change their perspective and revalidate whether current assumptions hold true.

- When entering a new market, brands should consider adapting their value propositions for each link in the Branded Product Value Chain.

Know Yourself, Know Your Enemy

- Understand competitive threats by getting inside the heads of your competitors. Ask yourself what problems are being solved for the end-user, how competitors are addressing those problems, and why the competition is choosing to solve those problems the way that they do.

- Use guerrilla-style research techniques like intercept interviews and market immersions to quickly unlock meaningful insights on your target.

- Triangulate, using several methods to approximate the "size of the prize," then reconcile differences to arrive at a reasonable estimate.

Get Lean and Mean

- Global brand builders can increase agility and speed to market by using a lean development process that includes rapid prototyping, co-creation, and ninja-style testing.

- Use the Lean Brand Canvas tool to create hypotheses for each brand-building block that together defines your total branded offering.

- Improve the quality of your innovation by "getting out of the building" and engaging in co-creation to build rapid prototypes and test your hypotheses with real end-users in real-life situations.

Choose Your Stance

- Identify the real needs that consumers are trying to solve when they decide between brands.

- Segment your competition based on their ability to meet those real consumer needs.

- Expose perceptual gaps in the competitive set and then select a differentiated positioning that you can own in the minds of consumers.

Adapt to Win

- When deciding what to adapt, drill down to those factors that will most likely influence consumers when they make their purchase decision.

- Amplify associations that enhance your brand's strengths and opportunities and minimize potential weaknesses and threats.

- Borrow brand equity from other brands to amplify or dampen existing perceptions.

Step Up and Disrupt

- Create a step-change in your brand's growth trajectory by riding disruptive technologies.

- Identify emerging technologies that have the potential to become a catalyst for faster growth.

- Assess each link in your branded product value chain to determine where you can leverage technology to exceed stakeholder expectations.

Make It Happen

- Before your message can genuinely inspire and rally a team, the messaging needs to be 1) on strategy; 2) memorable; and 3) presented in a format that can be easily adapted to remain relevant when being adapted by local teams.

- The brands we love change our lives for the better. For a brand to change lives, it has to address the real perceptions and problems of consumers.

- An effective brand story breaks through the competitive clutter by 1) grabbing the listener's attention; 2) sustaining that attention; and 3) giving the listener a reason to empathize with the brand. Consumers and stakeholders identify with brands that they perceive understand them.

Get Creative

- Neither pure logic nor pure intuition can achieve "creative genius." Creativity is a merged (analytical/heuristic) process that requires harnessing both the subconscious and conscious mind.

- The creative process starts with gathering knowledge and insights that refine your intuition. Then, your honed intuition can be used to generate innovative ideas.

- Creativity needs a jump-off point, so use empathetic, analog, systems, and springboard "creativity hacks" to help you generate innovative solutions.

Notes

Chapter 1

1. Igaueno Tourist Association, www.iganinja.jp.

2. Julian Ryall, "Top Ninja to Offer Classes for Businessmen," *The Telegraph* 6 (2012).

3. Antony Cummins, *In Search of the Ninja* (Cheltenham, UK: The History Press, 2016).

Chapter 2

1. "World's Population Increasingly Urban with More than Half Living in Urban Areas," United Nations, July 10 2014, www.un.org.

2. David Jin, et al., "Winning in Emerging-Market Cities," *BCG Report* (2010).

3. Abheek Singhi, Nimisha Jain, and Kanika Sanghi, "The New Indian: The Many Facets of a Changing Consumer," March 20, 2017, www.bcg.com.

4. Jacob Poushter, "Smartphone Ownership and Internet Usage Continues to Climb in Emerging Economies," February 22, 2016, www.pewglobal.org.

5. Frank Tong, "Online Retail Sales in China Soar Past $1 Trillion in 2017," February 8, 2018, www.digitalcommerce360.com.

6. "Affordable Luxury in Emerging and Developing Markets and the Impact," *Euromonitor International* (2016).

7. Nielsen Global Premiumization Report, 2016.

8. Matthew Eyring, Mark W. Johnson, Hari Nair, "New Business Models in Emerging Markets," *Harvard Business Review* (2011).

9. Saumya Tewari, "Average Indian Spends $1.8 Every Day; Chinese, $7," *IndiaSpend,* (2016).

10. P. Mulder, *Product Life Cycle Stages* (2012).

11. Ralf Leszinski and Michael Marn, "Setting Value, Not Price," *McKinsey Quarterly,* February 1997, www.mckinsey.com.

12. Lawrence R. Gustin, *Buick Motor Division, BMD—A Brief History,* 1993, www.buickclub.org.

13. "Buick Is a Lot More Than a Dad Wagon in China," *CNN Money,* February 22, 2017, www.money.cnn.com.

14. Andrew Jacobs and Adam Century, "In China, Car Brands Evoke an Unexpected Set of Stereotypes," *New York Times,* November 14, 2011, www.nytimes.com.

15. Janet Tu, "Starbucks Doubles Down on China Growth Hopes," *The Seattle Times,* April 21, 2016, www.seattletimes.com.

16. Paul Reynolds, "Countries Where Buying Starbucks Is the Most and Least Extravagant," *Value Penguin,* 2016, www.valuepenguin.com.

17. "Haagen-Dazs Feels the Heat in Smaller Cities," *China Daily Asia,* 2016.

18. "Haagen-Dazs Parlays Parlors into Success," *China Daily Asia,* 2009.

Chapter 3

1. Heisler Yoni, "How Apple Conducts Market Research and Keeps iOS Source Code Locked Down," August 3, 2012, www.network world.com.

2. Jon Fingas, "Apple Sees Its Redesigned Retail Stores as Community Spaces," April 25, 2017, www.endgadget.com.

3. Nick Statt, "Apple Just Revealed the Future of Its Retail Stores," *The Verge,* May 19, 2016.

4. Angela Ahrendts, "Another Exciting Chapter," LinkedIn December 27, 2017.

5. "Mondelēz International Improves Campaign Effectiveness with Google's Brand Lift Solution," October 2014, www.Thinkwith Google.com.

Chapter 4

1. IMF Data, March 10, 2018, www.imf.org.

2. Richard Dobbs, Jaana Remes, James Manyika, Charles Roxburgh, Sven Smit, and Fabian Schaer, "Urban World: Cities and the Rise of the Consumer Class, McKinsey & Company 2012," McKinsey Global Institute, June 2012, www.mckinsey.com.

3. "Looking to Achieve New Product Success?," Nielson Global New Product Innovation Report, June 2015, www.nielsen.com.

4. David Aaker, *Aaker on Branding: 20 Principles that Drive Success* (New York: Morgan James Publishing, 2014).

5. Tom Doctoroff, "What Is Value? Marketing to Consumers in Emerging Economies," August 13, 2017, www.HuffingtonPost.com.

6. Jesko Perrey, Tjark Freundt, and Dennis Spillecke, *The Brand Is Back: Staying Relevant in an Accelerating Age,* www.mckinsey. com, published May 2015, accessed March 10, 2018

7. Amos Winter and Vijay Govindarajan, "Engineering Reverse Innovations," *Harvard Business Review* (2015).

8. "Reverse Innovation: GE Makes India a Lab for Global Markets," May 20, 2010, www.upenn.edu.

9. Natalie Zmuda, "P&G, Levi's, GE Innovate by Thinking in Reverse," *AdAge,* June 13, 2011.

10. Rob Wengel, "How to Flip 85% Misses to 85% Hits: Lessons from the Nielsen Breakthrough Innovation Project," June 24, 2014, www.nielsen.com.

11. www.theleanstartup.com.

12. Todd Warren, "Getting the Most Out of 'Getting Out of the Building,'" *Forbes* (2013).

13. Steven Mullen, "An Introduction to Lean Canvas," *Medium* (2016).

14. Caryn Livingston, "Parcel, e-Commerce, Express Deliver Strong Q3 Results for DP-DHL," November 9, 2017, www.aircargo world.com.

15. "Inspire. Connect. Engage." March 10, 2018, www.dhl.com.

16. Christine Crandell, "Customer Co-Creation Is the Secret Sauce to Success," June 10, 2016, www.forbes.com.

17. "Best Global Brands," 2017, www.interbarnd.com.

18. Walter Loeb, "Zara's Secret to Success: The New Science of Retailing," October 14, 2013, www.forbes.com.

19. Eli Greenblat and Kelsey Munro, "Fashionably Fast the Key to Zara Success," *The Sydney Morning Herald*, March 9, 2013, www.smh.com.au.

20. Suzy Hansen, "How Zara Grew into the World's Largest Fashion Retailer," November 9, 2012, www.nytimes.com.

21. Greg Petro, "The Future of Fashion Retailing: The Zara Approach (Part 2 of 3)," October 25, 2012, www.forbes.com.

22. Nick DePaula, "How the Big Baller Brand Is Trying to Disrupt the Entire Sneaker Industry," August 4, 2017, www.espn.com.

23. Marc Bain, "Adidas Can Now Make Specialized Shoes for Runners in Different Cities, Thanks to Robots," October 4, 2017, www.qz.com.

24. "The Future of Fast Fashion: Adidas Is Launching a Customizable Footwear Factory," October 18, 2017, www.mashable.com.

Chapter 5

1. Panos Mourdoukoutas, "How Long Does It Take to Create a Brand?," April 21, 2014, www.Forbes.com.

2. Jeff Kauflin, "The Most Powerful Brands in 2017," February 14, 2017, www.Forbes.com.

3. "LEGO Brand Identity & Experience Guide," LEGO Group, 2014, www.hothbricks.com.

4. Jonathan E. Schroeder, *Brand Culture* (Miriam Salzer-Mörling, Søren Askegaard: Routledge, Taylor & Francis, 2006, 19).

5. UrbanDictionary.com.

6. Al Ries and Jack Trout, *Positioning: The Battle for Your Mind* (2000).

7. "Perceptual Mapping: A Manager's Guide," *Harvard Business Review* (1990).

8. "The History of the Levi's 501 Jeans," Levis Strauss Press Center, www.levistrauss.com.

9. Sallie Hofmeister, "Used American Jeans Power a Thriving Industry Abroad," August 22, 1994, www.nytimes.com.

10. Ed Levine, "Pizza: A Slice of Heaven," slice.seriouseats.com.

11. Brandon Gaille, "29 Great Pizza Consumption Statistics," May 23, 2017, brandongaille.com.

12. Rick Hynum, "Pizza Power 2017—A State of the Industry Report," *PMQ Pizza Magazine,* December 2016, www.pmq.com.

13. "Domino's Prices," www.fastfoodmenuprices.com.

14. Annette Ekin, "The Weird and Wonderful World of Korean Pizza," January 9, 2016, www.slate.com.

15. Annette Ekin, "The Weird and Wonderful World of Korean Pizza," April 4, 2017, www.explorepartsunknown.com.

16. "Statista," 2018, www.statista.com.

17. "Description of Minute Maid Concentrated Orange Juice Can," The National Museum of American History, americanhistory.si.edu/.

18. "China Disposable Income Per Capita," National Bureau of Statistics of China, www.tradingeconomics.com.

19. Vivian Ki, "Q&A with Vivian Ki: The Minute Maid Case," *China Business Knowledge,* December 11, 2013, www.baschool.cuhk.edu.hk.

20. Yuwei Zhang, "Coke's 2020 Vision for China," *China Daily,* May 7, 2011, www.chinadailyasia.com.

21. Rajiv Lal and Carin-Isabel Knoop, "The Universalization of L'Oreal," *Havard Business School,* November 5, 2012.

22. "The Evolution of Traditional Beauty Codes," www.loreal.com.

23. "L'Oreal Consumer Insight Study," *Beauty by Region,* www.loreal.com.

24. Trefis Team, "Why Is L'Oreal Increasing Its Focus on India?" October 20, 2015, www.forbes.com.

25. Jock Phillips, "Sports and Leisure: Organized Sports," *Te Ara—the Encyclopedia of New Zealand,* www.TeAra.govt.nz/.

26. Yang Liu, Yan Tang, Zhen-Bo Cao, Pei-Jie Chen, Jia-Lin Zhang, Zheng Zhu, Jie Zhuang, Yang Yang, and Yue-Ying Hu, "Results from Shanghai's (China) 2016 Report Card on Physical Activity for Children and Youth," *Journal of Physical Activity and Health* (2016).

27. Katherine Ryder, "China's Labor Market: Valuable Asset or Economic Albatross?" December 17, 2010, www.fortune.com.

28. "China Faces Employment Crisis; Recent Graduates, Rural Migrants Among Hardest Hit," *NDRC,* www.worldwatch.org.

29. Tibi Puiu, "Why Chinese Men Are the Most Single in the World: The Perils of Gender Imbalance in China," *ZME Science,* May 18, 2016, www.zmescience.com.

30. Rob Budden, "Why Millions of Chinese Men Are Staying Single," *Capital BBC,* February 14, 2017, www.bbc.com.

Chapter 6

1. "Moving On Up—Premium Products Are in High Demand Around the World," *Nielsen Global Premiumization Report,* December 2016.

2. Micah Maidenberg, "Nike Will Try Going Local by Focusing on 12 Cities," *New York Times,* June 16, 2017.

3. Michael Czinkota and Ilkka Ronkainen, "Achieving 'Glocal' Success," www.ama.org.

4. Nigel Hollis, "Global Brands and Local Culture, Market Leader," *The Journal of the Marketing Society,* July 9, 2012, www.marketingsociety.com.

5. Al Ries, "Having a Better Brand Is Better than Having a Better Product," *Ad Age,* September 5, 2014, www.adage.com.

6. Viren Swani, "Why Opposites Rarely Attract," *The Conversation,* March 24, 2017, www.theconversation.com.

7. Youyou Wu, "Couples, Friends Show Similarity in Personality Traits After All," *Association for Psychological Science,* February 11, 2017, www.psychologicalscience.org.

8. Archana Kumar and Youn-Kyung Kim, "The Store-as-a-Brand Strategy: The Effect of Store Environment on Customer Responses," *Journal of Retailing and Consumer Services* (2014).

9. Dirk Standen, "The Future of Shopping, Part Three: Mark Lee," November 13, 2014, www.vogue.com.

10. Lauren Sherman, "Inside the Business of Barneys New York," February, 12, 2016, www.businessoffashion.com.

11. "Innesfree Brand Story," 2018, www.innesfree.com.

12. Christina Tan, "South Korean Beauty Brand Amorepacific Looks to Global Expansion," May 26, 2017, www.cnbc.com.

13. www.sunnyhills.com.

14. Angela Kubo, "SunnyHills Taiwanese Pineapple Cakes," *The Japan Times,* January 7, 2018, www.japantimes.com.

15. David Hong, "China's Coffee Hit: Starbucks and Nestlé Dominate, but the Market Is Still Growing," July 19, 2013, www.Nasdaq.com.

16. Junqian Xu, "A Storm Brewing in the Coffee Cup," *China Daily USA*, January 9, 2016, www.chinadaily.com.

17. Reuters Staff, "Huawei Wants to Beat Apple in Smartphones in Two Years," *Reuters*, November 4, 2016, www.reuters.com.

18. Jessica Dong, *Western European Consumer Perception of a Chinese Brand. An Examination of Huawei* (Munich, Germany: GRIN, 2014).

19. "Here's How Huawei's Latest Bevy of Smartphones Undercut Apple and Samsung," October, 16, 2017, www.fortune.com.

20. Ted Marzilli, "Samsung Galaxy Recovers as the iPhone Stumbles," *YouGov US*, October 18, 2017, www.today.yougov.com.

21. www.en.leica-camera.com.

22. Laura Oswald, *Creating Value, The Theory and Practice of Marketing Semiotics Research* (United Kingdom: Oxford University Press, 2015).

23. Christine Birkner, "Coca-Cola and Pepsi Are Both Losing Millennial Fans," *ADWEEK*, December 5, 2016.

24. Danielle Long, "How Coca-Cola Is Targeting China's 355 Million Teens to Share a Coke," June 27, 2017, www.thedrum.com.

25. Heidi Han, "Luhan, the 'Chinese Justin Bieber' Crashes China's Social Networks Announcing New Relationship," October 9, 2017, www.sbs.com.au.

26. Yuval Atsmon, Jean-Frederic Kuentz, and Jeongmin Seong, "Building Brand in Emerging Markets," *McKinsey Quarterly* (2012).

27. Paul Howell, "Case Study: Dettol's Unique Word-of-Mouth Campaign in China," December 7, 2018, www.campaignasia.com.

28. Nielsen Brand-Origin Report, April 2016.

29. www.goldenbrown.info.

30. Tom Downey, "How Japan Copied American Culture and Made It Better," *Smithsonian Magazine,* April 2014, www.smithsonian.com.

31. Lucy Tesseras, "Beats CMO on Dr Dre, Ambassadors and Unconventional Marketing," *Marketing Week,* January, 14, 2016, www.marketingweek.com.

32. Social Brand Watch, "Beats by Dr. Dre Uses Chinese Celebrity Cool Kids to Promote Their 'Straight Outta' Campaign," November 12, 2015, www.socialbrandwatch.com.

33. www.showcase.pmg.com.

34. "Beats by Dre: Straight Outta Campaign," *Campaign Report,* November 11, 2015, www.resonamcechina.com.

35. Richard Wike, "6 Facts About How Americans and Chinese See Each Other," September 22, 2015, www.pewresearch.org.

36. Helen Wang, "China's Millennial Consumers: What Victoria's Secret Got Wrong, and Nike Got Right," December 22, 2016, www.Forbes.com.

37. Ying Yu, Huihui Sun, Steve Goodman, Shangwu Chen, and Huiqin Ma, "Chinese Choices: A Survey of Wine Consumers in Beijing," *International Journal of Wine Business Research* 21 (2009).

38. Martin Moodie, "The Martin Moodie Interview: Streamlined Diageo Targets Renewed Travel Retail Impetus," *The Moddie Davitt Report,* January 4, 2018.

39. Yigit Mumcu and Halil Semih Kimzan, "The Effect of Visual Product Aesthetics on Consumers' Price Sensitivity," 2015, www.ScienceDirect.com.

40. "Bling It On! What Makes a Millennial Spend More?" (The Creative Studio at Deloitte, 2017).

41. "Limited-edition Johnnie Walker Bottle Celebrates Year of the Dog," *Alcohol, Beverage, Industries, New Products, Packaging Print*, January 2, 2018, www.foodbev.com.

42. Cai Fengyan, Rajesh Bagchi, and Dinesh K. Gauri, "Boomerang Effects of Low Price Discounts: How Low Price Discounts Affect Purchase Propensity," *Journal of Consumer Research* 42, no. 5 (2016): 804–816.

43. "Identifying Growth Opportunities for Plastic Closures in Beauty and Home Care Global Briefing," blog.euromonitor.com.

44. Catalin Munteanu and Andreea Pagalea, *Brands as a Mean of Consumer Self-Expression and Desired Personal Lifestyle* (Amsterdam: Elsevier Ltd., 2014).

45. Wang Xuehua and Zhilin Yang, *The Impact of Brand Credibility and Brand Personality on Purchase Intention: An Empirical Study in China* (Bingley, United Kingdom: Emerald Group Publishing Limited, 2011), 137–153.

46. David Aaker, "How to Identify Your Brand Personality," 2017, www.prophet.com.

47. Christian Jarrett, "Different Nationalities Really Have Different Personalities," April 13, 2017, www.bbc.com.

48. Graham Staplehurst and Suthapa Charoenwongse, "Why Brand Personality Matters: Aligning Your Brand to Cultural Drivers of Success," 2012, www.millwardbrown.com.

49. Pamela Danzinger, "Nike to Stay Out in Front with Biggest Data of All: Demographics," June 19, 2017, www.forbes.com.

50. Yuval Atsmon and Max Magni, "Chinese Consumers: Revisiting Our Predictions," *McKinsey Quarterly* (2016).

51. Kate Abnett, "Business of Fashion," www.businessoffashion.com.

52. "We Are More Different Than You Think: A Look at the Diversity of Millennial Ideas and Attitudes Within Regions, and the Implications for Employers," www.universumglobal.com.

53. Georgina Caldwell, "Shiseido to Target Millennials with New Brand Recipist," December 6, 2017, www.globalcosmeticsnews.com.

54. Motokazu Matsui and Nana Shibata, "Shiseido Fights Its Way Back into Millennials' Makeup Pouches," *Nikkei Asian Review* (2017).

55. "New Brand 'Recipist' Created in Collaboration with the Millennials Who Live Each Day with Care," Shiseido Advertising and Design Departments, January 2018, www.shiseidogroup.com.

56. "On 'Kawaii' and the Power of Cute: Let's Put a Face on It," www.merriamwebster.com.

57. Joshua Dale, "The Ultimate Act of Love? The Truth Behind Japan's Charaben Culture," *CNN Travel*, March 15, 2017, www.cnn.com.

58. Lucy Tandon Copp, "Shiseido Recruits 'High School Girls' to Create New POSME Brand," January 17, 2017, www.cosmetics business.com.

59. Lily Bradic, "Celebrity Endorsements on Social Media Are Driving Sales and Winning Over Fans, Social Media Week," September 30, 2015, www.socialmediaweek.com.

60. Minmin Wang, "How to Select the Right Celebrity Endorser?" January 1, 2017, www.ipsos.com.

61. "Carmakers Turn to TV Drama for Killer Promotions," November 25, 2012, www.koreaherald.com.

62. "Korean Drama Review: My Love from Another Star," March 24, 2017, www.beelinelanguage.com.

63. "IKEA, Business Concept, Vision and Business Idea," August 31, 2016, www.ikea.com.

64. Stefan Svensson, "The Role of the New IKEA Catalogue," Inter IKEA Systems, B.V. Media Production, 2012.

65. Beth Kowitt, "How IKEA Took Over the World," March 15, 2015, www.fortune.com.

66. Annabel Fenwick Elliott, "Smaller Kitchens in China and Photoshopped Appliances: How IKEA Adapts Its Catalogues to Suit Different Cultures Around the World," *Mail Online,* August 2, 2017, www.dailymail.co.uk.

67. Anne Quito, "How the IKEA Catalogue Cracked What 'Domestic Bliss' Means in Different Cultures," July 25, 2017, www.Quartz.qz.com.

68. Geoffrey James, "20 Epic Fails in Global Branding," October 29, 2014, www.Inc.com.

69. Benjamin Koellmann, "Smart Cookie," March 31, 2013, www.businesstoday.com.

70. Jonathan Kaimen, "How the Humble KitKat Conquered Japan with Ever-Changing Flavors. Anyone for Sushi KitKat?," December 12, 2017, www.latimes.com.

71. Phaedra Cook, "Why Japanese KitKat Bars Are Coveted in the United States," July 28, 2016, www.houstonpress.com.

72. "Nestlé's Ruby Chocolate Debuts in Japan with KitKats, Just in Time for Valentine's Day," January, 18, 2018.

73. Geoffrey Fowler, "Starbucks' Road to China," *The Wall Street Journal* (2003).

74. "More Than Advertisement—IMC Case of Starbucks in China," Deakin Business School Marketing Management Blog, May 8, 2016.

75. "Our Mission and Values," www.starbucks.com.

76. Russell Flannery, "Meet The Woman Behind Starbucks' Rapid Growth in China," March 2017, www.forbes.com.

77. "Starbucks China Thrives with WeChat Partnership," *Inside Retail Hong Kong,* published May 11, 2017, www.insiderretail.hk.

78. Scott Cendrowski, "Tesla Makes a U-Turn in China," June 15, 2017, www.fortune.com.

79. Evie Liu, "Why Tesla's Cars Cost 50% More in China," April 14, 2017, www.barrons.com.

80. Danny King, "Tesla Reaching Kids at China 'Experience Centers,'" June 1, 2016, www.autoblog.com.

81. Eric Jhonsa, "Tesla Is Following Apple's Lead in China," October 24, 2017, www.thestreet.com.

Chapter 7

1. Clayton M. Christensen, Michael E. Raynor, and Rory McDonald, "What Is Disruptive Innovation?," *Harvard Business Review,* (2015).

2. "The Interstate Highway System," A+E Networks, 2010, *www.history.com.*

3. "Average Growth Rate For Startups," November 30, 2016, www.equidam.com.

4. "S&P 500 Sales Growth Rate," www.multpl.com.

5. "Tesla Q4 2017 Vehicle Production and Deliveries," January 3, 2018, www.nasdaq.com.

6. Leigh Gallagher, "Airbnb's Profits to Top $3 Billion by 2020," February 15, 2017, www.fortune.com.

7. Eric Newcomer, "Uber, Lifting Financial Veil, Says Sales Growth Outpaces Losses," April 15, 2017, www.Bloomberg.com.

8. "The CMO Survey," February 2017, www.cmosurvey.com.

9. "Gartner Says 8.4 Billion Connected 'Things' Will Be in Use in 2017, Up 31 Percent from 2016," January 2017, www.gartner.com.

10. "A Guide to the Internet of Things Infographic," www.intel.com.

11. Roger Slavens, "ME Alumni, Coca-Cola Freestyle Winning Formula," *Georgia Tech Alumni* magazine, 2019, www.me.gatech.edu.

12. Jay Moye, "Fountain Favorite: Sprite Cherry Is First National Brand Inspired by Coca-Cola Freestyle," February 13, 2017, www.coca-colacompany.com.

13. Hugh Locke, "Smallholder Farmers Are the New Global Food Frontier," August 27, 2015, www.huffingtonpost.com.

14. www.eastwestseed.com.

15. Lee Rainie and Andrew Perrin, "10 Facts About Smartphones as the iPhone Turns 10," Pew Research Center, June 28, 2017.

16. Simon Kemp, "The Full Guide to Southeast Asia's Digital Landscape in 2017," Tech In Asia, February 8, 2017, www.tech inasia.com.

17. David Smith, "Internet Use on Mobile Phones in Africa Predicted to Increase 20-Fold," June 5, 2014, www.thegaurdian.com.

18. Santosh Maharshi, "Gray Matrix Software Projects—A Quick Portfolio, Gray Matrix," September 22, 2017, gm360.in.

19. www.mccainindia.com.

20. Vaishali Gauba, "India's Fast-Food Industry Is Becoming a Major Market," April 2, 2015, www.cnbc.com.

21. "McDonald's India: Optimizing the French Fries Supply Chain, Case: GS-79," Stanford Graduate School of Business, November 19, 2013.

22. Stephen Belyea, "Commercial Potato Production in North America," *The Potato Association of America Handbook* (2010).

23. "Using Technology for Complete Farm Management," McCain Case Study, February 5, 2018, www.Cropin.co.in.

24. "Radio Frequency Identification (RFID): What Is It?" April 25, 2017, www.dhs.gov.

25. "Seven-Eleven Japan Co. Ltd. 7-11 Around the World," December 31, 2017, www.sej.co.jp.

26. Preston Phro, "Looking for a Job in Japan? Try a Convenience Store," December 28, 2015, japantoday.com.

27. Akiko Katayama, February 26, 2019, www.Forbes.com.

28. "Japanese C-Stores to Offer Faster Checkout Technology, Convenience Store Decisions," April 24, 2017, www.cstoredecisions.com.

29. "Tesco Sells South Korea Stores for £4bn," BBC News, September 7, 2015, www.bbc.com.

30. Lee Hana, "Korea Has Highest Smartphone Ownership Rate," February 24, 2016, www.korea.net.

31. Martin Petit de Meurville, "Shop on the Go," *Business Today* (2015).

32. Yuan Yang and Yingzhi Yang, "Bike-Sharer Ofo Raises $1 Billion from Investors Including Alibaba," *Financial Times*, December 7, 2017, www.ft.com.

33. Sherisse Pham, "Chinese Bike-Sharing Startup Ofo Went Global. Now It May Go Bust," December 21, 2018, www.cnn.com.

34. www.salesforce.com.

35. www.salesforce.com.

36. Kevin Vasconi, "Domino's Delivers Explosive Growth with Cisco-Driven Digital Transformation," Cisco Domino's Case Study, www.cisco.com.

37. "Domino's Australia Uncovers the Full Value of Mobile Ads," November 2013, www.thinkwithgoogle.com.

38. "Domino's Makes Ordering from Google Home Even Easier," *PR Newswire* (2017).

39. "Domino's SMS, Emoji Ordering Goes Live," *Inside Retail*, December 14, 2015, www.insideretail.com.au.

40. George Nott, "Domino's Strong Growth Down to Tech Innovations," February 15, 2017, www.cio.com.au.

41. Andrew Griffin, "Apple's Tim Cook on iPhones, Augmented Reality, and How He Plans to Change Our World," October 10, 2017, www.independent.co.uk.

42. Lauren Indvik, "Exclusive: Apple's Tim Cook on the Future of Fashion & Shopping," October 11, 2017, www.vogue.co.uk.

43. Alec Banks, "5 of the Best Instances of Augmented Reality in Fashion & Retail," July 25, 2016, www.highsnobiety.com.

44. Sophia Markoulakis, "For Your Eyes (and Face) Only," *San Francisco Chronicle*, November 16, 2017, www.sfchronichle.com.

45. Gina Acosta, "For Sephora, Experience Matters," July 12, 2017, www.retailleader.com.

46. Jacqueline Renfrow, "Sephora Opens Beauty TIP Concept Stores in NYC," April 4, 2017, www.fierceretail.com.

47. Julie Naughton, "Sephora Unveils Beauty TIP Workshop Concept Store," November 17, 2015, www.wwd.com.

48. Nicholas Brautiecht, "IKEA Gambles on City-Xentre Store," *Financial Review*, July 1, 2014, www.afr.com.

49. "Five of the Best IKEA Marketing Campaigns Ever," www.appnova.com.

50. Aaron Luber, "What Virtual Reality Will Mean for Advertising," Think with Google, June 2016, www.thinkwithgoogle.com.

51. John Gaudiosi, "Patrón Is Using Virtual Reality to Market Tequila. Here's How," May 13, 2015, www.fortune.com.

52. "EON Reality's AVR Platform Makes Virtual Reality and Augmented Reality Application Development Easy and Strengthens the Man and Machine Connection," April 4, 2017, www.eonreality.com.

53. Eon Reality Inaugurates Interactive Digital Centre in Tshwane, South Africa," June 23, 2016, www.techsmart.co.za.

54. "Mondly Launches the First VR Language App with Speech Recognition on Daydream," ATi Studios, September 7, 2017, blog.mondlylanguages.com.

55. Robert Lee Hotz, "Drones Deliver Medical Supplies to Remote Areas," *The Wall Street Journal*, December 1, 2017, www.wsj.com.

56. Liz Jassin and Melia Robinson, "This Blood Delivery Saving Lives in Remote Areas," December 19, 2017, www.businessinsider.com.

57. Eliza Strickland, "Africa Leads the World on Drone Delivery: Flights to Begin in Tanzania in 2018," *IEEE Spectrum*, August 14, 2017, www. Spectrum.ieee.org.

58. Eliza Strickland, "New 'Ultrasound on a Chip' Tool Could Revolutionize Medical Imaging," *IEEE Spectrum*, October 27, 2017, www. Spectrum.ieee.org.

59. Oliver Pickup, "How Worldwide Businesses Should Prepare for the Rise of Artificial Intelligence," July 25, 2018, www.telegraph.co.uk.

60. "Sentient Technologies Raises $103.5 Million in Series C Funding," *Business Wire*, November 24, 2014, www.businesswire.com.

61. "Indian Farmers Use AI to Increase Crop Yields," February 12, 2018, borgenproject.org.

62. Amit Dua, "Budget 2018: How Will Artificial Intelligence Fuel the Indian Economy," February 6, 2018, yourstory.com.

63. "Microsoft AI Helping Indian Farmers Increase Crop Yields," December 17, 2017, economictimes.indiatimes.com.

64. "Digital Agriculture: Farmers in India Are Using AI to Increase Crop," *Microsoft News Center India,* February 18, 2018, news .microsoft.com.

65. "Gartner Survey Reveals That High Acquisition and Start-Up Costs Are Delaying Investment in 3D Printers," December 9, 2014, www.gartner.com.

66. Jason Hook, "China's 3D Printed Apartments," November 25, 2016, www.buildsoft.com.au.

67. Rory Scott, "Chinese Company Showcases Ten 3-D Printed Houses," September 2, 2014, www.archdaily.com.

68. "Aecom Forms Alliance with Chinese 3D Printer WinSun," May 19, 2017, www.globalconstructionreview.com.

69. Ian Birrell, "The Promise of 3-D Printing Body Parts," February, 22, 2017, www.theatlantic.com.

70. "Expo for Design Innovation and Technology," Press Release, July 19, 2017.

71. www.niatech.org.

Chapter 8

1. Eric Jackson, "Sun Tzu's 31 Best Pieces of Leadership Advice," May 23, 2014, www.forbes.com.

2. us.moleskine.com.

3. www.hsbc.com.

4. michiny.com.

5. Dave Bartosiak. "Dream Car Survey Reveals Americans Love American Cars," January 31, 2018, www.thedrive.com.

6. Robert Cumberford, "2018 Design of the Year: Tesla Model 3," February 22, 2018, www.autromobilemag.com.

7. bluebottlecoffee.com.

8. starbucks.com.

9. Michael Pooler and Peggy Hollinger, "Dyson's Perfectionists Invent a Future Beyond Vacuum Cleaners," February 8, 2017, www.ft.com.

10. Adam Satariano, "Dyson's Latest Cordless Vacuums Drive Sales Past $3 Billion," March 27, 2017, www.bloomberg.com.

11. www.dyson.com.

12. Elaine Watson, "Fairlife Ultra-Filtered Milk Sales Grew 79% in 2016," February 24, 2018, www.foodnavigator-usa.com.

13. www.dyson.com.

14. Ray Latif, "Coke-Backed Fairlife Milk Goes National," February 3, 2015, www.bevnet.com.

15. Lani Peterson, "The Science Behind the Art of Storytelling," November 14, 2017, www.harvardbusiness.org.

16. Jeremy Donovan, *How to Deliver a TED Talk: Secrets of the World's Most Inspiring Presentations* (New York: McGraw-Hill Education, 2013).

17. Greg J. Stephens, Lauren J. Silbert, and Uri Hasson. "Speaker–Listener Neural Coupling Underlies Successful Communication," *Proceedings of the National Academy of Sciences of the United States of America* 107.32 (2010): 14425–14430.

18. Joshua Gowin, "Why Sharing Stories Brings People Together," February 25, 2018, ww.psychologytoday.com.

19. John Medina, *Brain Rules (Updated and Expanded): 12 Principles for Surviving and Thriving at Work, Home, and School* (Seattle: Pear Press, 2014).

20. "2017 Businessolver Workplace Empathy Monitor Executive Summary," *Businessolver Workplace Empathy Monitor* (2017).

21. www.toms.com.

22. www.burtsbees.com.

23. *Burt's Bees Corporate Social Responsibility Report*, 2017, issuu.com.

24. www.clifbar.com.

25. www.johnniewalker.com.

26. Afshin Molavi, "Straight Up: How Johnnie Walker Conquered the World," December 8, 2013, www.post-gazette.com.

27. Eli Epstine, "The Johnnie Walker Brand: A Rich Blend of Design and Progress," May 2, 2014, www.mashable.com.

28. www.stock.walmart.com.

29. Beth Kowitt, "When It Comes to Purpose, Walmart Returns to Its Roots," October 13, 2015, www.fortune.com.

30. Peter Fisk, *Creating Innovative Strategies for Business and Brands; New Approaches to Strategy, Innovation and Marketing* (Hoboken, NJ: John Wiley & Sons, 2014), 46.

31. Drake Baer, "Timelness Branding Lessons from a Young Steve Jobs," August 12, 2013, www.fastcompany.com.

32. Apple Computer, Inc., www.thecrazyones.it/.

33. Rob Siltanen, "The Real Story Behind Apple's 'Think Different' Campaign," December 14, 2011, www.forbes.com.

34. Scott Thompson, "Ninja Energy Meditation Techniques," August 14, 2017, www.livestrong.com.

35. Carmen Nobel, "The Power of Rituals in Life, Death, and Business," June 3, 2013, https://hbswk.hbs.edu.

36. "The Power of Rituals in Eating, Grieving and Business," *HBS Working Knowledge*, June 3, 2013, www.forbes.com.

37. www.clinique.jobs.com.

38. P. Lally, C. H. M. van Jaarsveld, H. W. W. Potts, and J. Wardle, "How Are Habits Formed: Modeling Habit Formation in the Real World," *European Journal of Social Psychology* 40 (2010): 998–1009.

39. Thomas C. Frohlich and Alexander Kent, "These Are the 10 Oldest Logos in the World," June 20, 2014, www.time.com.

40. https://piercebrennandesign.wordpress.com

41. "Meet the Stella Artois Draught Masters," December 13, 2011, www.morningadvertiser.co.uk.

42. Melissa Dowing, "The Fastest Growing Beer Brands of 2016," October 16, 2017, www.beveragedynamics.com.

43. Andrea Navarro, "America's Thirst for Corona Helps Mexico Dominate Beer Imports," February 16, 2018, www.bloomberg.com.

44. www.marketinomics.com.

45. "How Subliminal Advertising Works," January 4, 2009, https://parade.com.

46. www.goodreads.com.

47. Mindi Chahal, "How to Make Global Marketing Locally Relevant," February 26, 2015, www.maeketingweek.com.

48. www.unilver.com.

49. "Establishing Global Brand Consistency," https://percolate.com.

50. "The Hub Network Fuels Coke's Real-Time Marketing," November 3, 2014, www.coca-colacompany.com.

51. Seb Joseph, "Coca-Cola Centralises Social Media Marketing," October 18, 2016, www.thedrum.com.

52. "Drive Engagement on Social Media with Coca-ColaFreestyle," June 1, 2016, www.cokesolutions.com.

Chapter 9

1. Kobi Ledor, ledorfineart.com.

2. Carolyn Sun, "How Do Your Reading Habits Compare to Elon Musk's, Mark Zuckerberg's and Warren Buffett's?," December 1, 2017, www.entrepreneur.com.

3. Elle Kaplan, "How to Use the Reading Habits of Billionaires to Radically Improve Your Intelligence and Success," November 21, 2016, www.medium.com.

4. Daniel H. Pink, *Drive: The Surprising Truth About What Motivates Us* (New York: Riverhead Books, 2011).

5. William Hermanns, *Einstein and the Poet: In Search of the Cosmic Man* (Wellesley, MA: Branden Publishing Company, 1983).

6. Daniel Cappon, "The Anatomy of Intuition," May 1993, www.psychologytoday.com.

7. David DiSalvo, "Your Brain Sees Even When You Don't," June 22, 2013, www.forbes.com.

8. "How Unconscious Processing Improves Decision-Making," *ScienceDaily* (2013).

9. Ozcan Saygin, Kemal Goral, Halil Ibrahim Ceylan, and Mugla Sitki, "An Examination of the Coincidence Anticipation Performance of Soccer Players According to Their Playing Positions and Different Stimulus Speeds," *The Sport Journal*, August 18, 2016, www.thesportjournal.org.

10. Ted Kardash, "Taoism—Ancient Wisdom for a Modern World: The Tao of Daily Living," March 18, 2018, www.pacificcol lege.edu.

11. Christina Sarich, "Bruce Lee's Taoist Wisdom," February 14, 2017, www.themindunleashed.com.

12. Brian White, "A Five Minute Introduction," www.budahnet.net.

13. www.unidhi.org.au.

14. Joel Webber, "What Leonardo da Vinci and Steve Jobs Have in Common: Walter Isaacson's New Biography of the Creative Genius Offers Insights for Business Leaders Today," October 18, 2017, www.bloomberg.com.

15. Ruth Umoh, "Steve Jobs and Albert Einstein Both Attributed Their Extraordinary Success to This Personality Trait," June 29, 2017, www.cnbc.com.

16. Michele and Robert Root-Bernstein, "Einstein on Creative Thinking: Music and the Intuitive Art of Scientific Imagination," March 31, 2010, www.psychologytoday.com.

17. Alice Calaprice, *The Ultimate Quotable Einstein* (Princeton, NJ: Princeton University Press and The Hebrew University of Jerusalem, 2011).

18. Maria Popova, "Einstein, Anne Lamott, and Steve Jobs on Intuition vs. Rationality," January 12, 2012, www.theatlantic.com.

19. Dan Farber, "What Steve Jobs Really Meant When He Said 'Good Artists Copy; Great Artists Steal,'" January 28, 2015, www.cnet.com.

20. Gregory Ferenstein, "Steve Jobs Biographer: Apple Founder Was Driven by Simplicity, Mystical Thinking, and Occasional LSD Use," October 26, 2011, www.fastcompany.com.

21. Larry Dignan, "Amazon CEO Jeff Bezos's 2017 Annual Letter: What Decision-Makers Can Learn," April 12, 2017, www.zdnet.com.

22. Danielle Abril, "Uber Eats Its Way to New Revenues Amid Post-IPO Profitability Concerns," May 14, 2019, www.Forbes.com.

23. Paul Clayton Smith, "How We Design on the UberEATS Team: Creating the Future of Food Delivery Takes Empathy, Innovation, and an Appetite for Complex Logistical Challenges," July 7, 2017, www.medium.com.

24. Burt Helm, "How I Did It: James Dyson," February 28, 2012, www.inc.com.

25. Mary Bellis, "The History of the iPhone," June 27, 2017, www.thoughtco.com.

26. www.linkedin.com.

27. Sarah Yager, "Doritos Locos Tacos," July/August 2014, www.theatlantic.com.

28. Andrus Aubre, "Inside Taco Bell's Innovation Lab," November 2016, www.qsrmagazine.com.

29. www.brainyquote.com.

Index

About the Author

Luis Pedroza has an MBA in marketing from the University of Southern California and is a Consortium for Graduate Study in Management fellow.

Luis is an expert at launching global brands and adapting global platforms to meet the needs of local markets. His passion for global marketing inspired him to take leadership positions with iconic global brands such as 7-Eleven, P&G, General Mills, and Nestlé.

His brand-building journey took him all over the world to live and work in many international markets including the United States, China, Russia, United Kingdom, and Singapore. He is living and working in the disruptive innovation capital of the world, the San Francisco Bay Area. All of this experience has shaped his view of the world and given him a very valuable perspective on what it takes to succeed in global marketing. Now, he wants to give back and inspire the next generation of global brand builders with this book.